FULL STACK DEVELOPMENT WITH SPRING BOOT 3 AND REACT

A Hands-On Guide to Building Scalable and Efficient Web Applications

SHARON J. MOORE

Sharon J. Moore is a passionate software developer and technology educator with over ten years of experience in Full Stack Web Development. She specializes in using cutting-edge technologies like Spring Boot and React to build scalable, high-performance web applications. Sharon has worked in a variety of roles, from backend engineering to UI/UX design, giving her a well-rounded understanding of the full stack.

Sharon is committed to helping both beginner and advanced developers enhance their coding skills through hands-on learning. She has contributed to several tech blogs, created online courses, and regularly speaks at developer conferences on topics like Spring Boot, React, and full stack development alongside several other Tech-based topics.

When she's not coding or writing, Sharon enjoys mentoring aspiring developers and exploring new technologies that push the boundaries of web application development.

GRATITUDE PAGE

Thank you so much for purchasing Full Stack Development with Spring Boot 3 and React! Your support means the world to me. I've poured my passion and expertise into this book to help you master full stack development and build powerful, scalable web applications. I truly hope the knowledge shared here empowers you to take your skills to the next level. If you found this book helpful, I'd greatly appreciate your feedback and a review—it helps others make informed decisions and allows me to keep improving. Wishing you all the best on your development journey!

This Book Belongs to:

_____

_____

_____

_____

Acknowledgments

I would like to express my deepest gratitude to everyone who made this book possible. To my family and friends, thank you for your unwavering support and encouragement. To my mentors and colleagues, your guidance has been invaluable in shaping my understanding of full stack development. A special thanks to the developers and educators who inspired me with their passion and expertise. Finally, to the readers—thank you for your commitment to learning and growing as developers. I hope this book helps you on your journey to mastering full stack development with Spring Boot 3 and React.

TABLE OF CONTENTS

PART 1

BACKEND DEVELOPMENT WITH SPRING BOOT 3

INTRODUCTION

WELCOME TO FULL STACK DEVELOPMENT

Full stack development combines the art and science of building both the frontend (user interface) and backend (server-side logic) of web applications. It's a highly valued skill in today's technology-driven world, enabling developers to create dynamic, scalable, and robust applications. This book introduces you to the powerful combination of Spring Boot 3 and React, two of the most popular tools for building modern web applications.

Importance of Full Stack Skills

In an era where businesses rely on web applications to engage customers and streamline operations, being a full stack developer is more important than ever. Here's why full stack development is a game-changing skill:

Versatility and Flexibility

Full stack developers can contribute to every stage of software development, from designing interactive user interfaces to deploying backend services. This flexibility makes them invaluable in any development team.

Efficient Problem Solving

By understanding the complete system, full stack developers can quickly diagnose and resolve issues involving both frontend and backend components, saving time and resources.

Cost-Effectiveness for Organizations

Companies benefit from hiring developers who can handle multiple layers of an application, reducing the need for separate specialists and improving team efficiency.

Demand in the Job Market

Full stack developers are among the most sought-after professionals in the tech industry. Their ability to bridge design and implementation makes them indispensable for creating high-quality applications.

Comprehensive Understanding of Web Applications

Mastering full stack development provides a holistic view of web applications, empowering developers to build cohesive, scalable, and maintainable solutions.

Why Spring Boot 3 and React?

Spring Boot 3: Powering the Backend

Spring Boot simplifies Java-based backend development by eliminating boilerplate code and offering powerful features:

Simplifies Backend Development: Provides pre-configured templates for faster coding.

Support for Microservices: Ideal for building modular and scalable systems.

Enterprise-Grade Security: Seamless integration with Spring Security for robust authentication and authorization.

Future-Ready: Enhanced performance, compatibility with Java 17, and support for frameworks like GraalVM.

React: Building the Frontend

React, backed by Facebook, is a widely adopted library for creating dynamic and interactive user interfaces:

Fast and Interactive UIs: Component-based architecture and virtual DOM for high performance.

Rich Ecosystem: Vast community and libraries for extending functionality.

Reusable Components: Modular design for code efficiency.

Seamless Integration: Works effortlessly with RESTful APIs created in Spring Boot.

Together, Spring Boot 3 and React provide a powerful combination for developing full stack applications that are scalable, efficient, and easy to maintain.

Who Is This Book For?

This book caters to a wide audience:

Beginners: Individuals with basic programming knowledge will find step-by-step instructions and examples to kickstart their journey.

Intermediate Developers: Those familiar with either backend or frontend development can expand their skill set to become proficient full stack developers.

Advanced Developers: Experienced professionals will explore advanced concepts, best practices, and modern techniques to build scalable applications.

Technology Enthusiasts: Anyone passionate about web technologies will gain hands-on experience in building efficient, production-ready applications.

How to Use This Book

This book is structured to guide you from foundational concepts to advanced topics. Here's how to maximize its value:

Follow Chapters Sequentially: Beginners should start from the basics, while experienced developers can jump to sections of interest.

Hands-On Learning: Practice with coding exercises, examples, and real-world projects included in each chapter.

Leverage Resources: Use supplementary materials, code repositories, and tools provided throughout the book to deepen your understanding.

Engage with Projects: The projects are designed to simulate real-world challenges, preparing you for actual development scenarios.

Adapt to Your Learning Style: Whether you prefer comprehensive reading or focusing on specific topics, this book accommodates all learning preferences.

Practice Consistently: Full stack development requires regular practice. Use the exercises and projects to refine your skills.

Setting Up Your Development Environment

A robust development environment is essential for full stack development. This book provides detailed guidance on setting up tools for Spring Boot 3 and React to ensure seamless development.

Tools and Software Required

Backend:

- Java Development Kit (JDK 17 or later)
- Spring Boot CLI (optional)
- Maven or Gradle (for dependency management)

Frontend:

- Node.js and npm (or Yarn)
- Modern browsers like Chrome or Firefox

General Tools:

- IDEs like IntelliJ IDEA or VS Code
- Version control systems like Git and platforms like GitHub or GitLab

Installing Spring Boot 3 and React

Spring Boot 3

Install JDK 17 or later from Oracle or OpenJDK.

Optionally install Spring Boot CLI for streamlined project setup.

Verify installations with:

```
java -version
spring --version
```

React

Install Node.js and npm from Node.js.

Create a React project using:

Setting Up Node.js and React

Step 1: Installing Node.js

Download Node.js:

Visit Node.js and download the **LTS (Long-Term Support)** version.

Install Node.js:

Follow the instructions for your operating system. Ensure npm (Node Package Manager) is installed along with Node.js.

Verify Installation:

```
node -v
npm -v
```

Step 2: Setting Up React

1.Create a React Project:

Use **create-react-app** or modern tools like Vite to initialize a React project:

```bash
Copy code
npx create-react-app my-react-app
```

OR with Vite:

```bash
Copy code
npm create vite@latest my-react-app
```

2.Navigate to the Project Directory:

```bash
Copy code
cd my-react-app
```

3.Start the Development Server:

```bash
```

```
Copy code
npm start
```

Your React app will be accessible at
http://localhost:3000.

IDE Recommendations

IntelliJ IDEA

Ideal for backend development with built-in Spring Boot support.

Download the Community Edition (free) or Ultimate Edition (paid).

Visual Studio Code (VS Code)

Lightweight and versatile, excellent for React projects.

Install extensions like Java Extension Pack, Prettier, and React Developer Tools for a seamless workflow.

Troubleshooting Tip.

Java Issues: Ensure `JAVA_HOME` is set correctly.

Node.js Errors: Use a version manager like `nvm` to resolve installation conflicts.

Port Conflicts: Free port 3000 with: `npx kill-port 3000`

By the end of this book, you will have mastered the tools, techniques, and best practices for building production-ready full stack applications. Let's dive in and start coding!

NOTES

CHAPTER 1

GETTING STARTED WITH SPRING BOOT 3

Spring Boot 3 is a robust and developer-friendly framework designed to streamline Java-based application development. It is built on the foundational principles of the Spring Framework, offering tools and features to simplify configuration, deployment, and scalability. This chapter introduces the Spring Framework, highlights the latest enhancements in Spring Boot 3, and walks you through creating your first Spring Boot application.

Introduction to Spring Framework

The **Spring Framework** is a comprehensive and modular Java-based framework used to build modern enterprise applications. It provides powerful tools for dependency injection, aspect-oriented programming, and seamless integration with various technologies. Key characteristics of the Spring Framework include:

1. Modular Architecture

The Spring Framework is divided into modules (e.g., Core, Data Access, Web, Security) that can be used independently or together. This modularity allows developers to pick only the components they need, reducing overhead.

2. Dependency Injection (DI)

At the core of Spring lies DI, a design pattern that promotes loose coupling between components. DI simplifies object creation and management, making applications easier to maintain and scale.

3. Aspect-Oriented Programming (AOP)

AOP provides a way to handle cross-cutting concerns (e.g., logging, security) separately from business logic, resulting in cleaner code.

4. Extensive Ecosystem

Spring integrates with a wide range of technologies, including Hibernate, JPA, Kafka, and RabbitMQ, enabling developers to build versatile applications.

The Spring Framework's versatility and robustness have made it a popular choice for building enterprise-grade applications, but its complexity often posed challenges, especially for newcomers. Enter **Spring Boot**, a subproject of Spring designed to simplify and accelerate development.

What's New in Spring Boot 3

Spring Boot 3 introduces several exciting features and improvements aimed at enhancing performance, compatibility, and developer productivity. Here are the highlights:

1. Compatibility with Java 17

Spring Boot 3 supports the latest Long-Term Support (LTS) version of Java (Java 17), bringing new language features like pattern matching, sealed classes, and enhanced performance.

2. GraalVM Native Image Support

Spring Boot 3 provides first-class support for building native images using GraalVM. Native images offer faster startup times and lower memory consumption, making them ideal for microservices and cloud environments.

3. Jakarta EE Migration

Spring Boot 3 has fully transitioned from Java EE (javax.) to Jakarta EE (jakarta.). This aligns the framework with the latest standards in enterprise Java development.

4. Improved Observability

Enhanced integration with Micrometer and OpenTelemetry for better application monitoring and observability. Developers can now gain deeper insights into application performance and health.

5. Enhanced Security Features

Spring Boot 3 includes updated security features with better support for OAuth 2.0 and OpenID Connect (OIDC), making it easier to secure applications.

6. Kotlin 1.7 Support

Kotlin support has been updated, allowing developers to leverage Kotlin's expressive syntax and null safety in Spring Boot applications.

7. New Property Binding Enhancements

Simplified configuration with improvements to property binding, making it easier to handle complex configuration scenarios.

Spring Boot 3 represents a significant leap forward, combining modern Java features with robust tools to build efficient and scalable applications.

Building Your First Spring Boot Application

Let's create a simple Spring Boot application to demonstrate its ease of use and setup.

Step 1: Set Up Your Environment

Before starting, ensure you have the following installed:

- **Java 17 or later**: Verify with `java -version`
- **Maven or Gradle**: Verify with `mvn -version` or `gradle -v`.
- **An IDE**: IntelliJ IDEA or Eclipse is recommended.

Step 2: Create a New Spring Boot Project

1.Using Spring Initializr:

Go to [Spring Initializr](#).

Choose the following settings:

- **Project**: Maven
- **Language:** Java
- **Spring Boot:** 3.x.x (latest stable release)
- **Dependencies:** Spring Web

Click **Generate** to download the project as a `.zip` file.

Extract the file and open it in your IDE.

2.Using CLI (Optional): If you have the Spring Boot CLI installed, you can create a project with:

```
spring    init    --dependencies=web    my-first-
spring-boot-app
cd my-first-spring-boot-app
```

Step 3: Understand the Project Structure

A typical Spring Boot project contains the following:

- **src/main/java**: Contains application source code.
- **src/main/resources**: Holds configuration files like `application.properties`.
- **pom.xml**: The Maven build file for managing dependencies.

Step 4: Write Your First Controller

Create a new file called in the `HelloController.java` `com.example.demo` Package:

```
package com.example.demo:

import
org.springframework.web.bind.annotation.GetMapping;
import
org.springframework.web.bind.annotation.RestControll
er;

@RestController
public class HelloController {

    @GetMapping("/hello")
    public String sayHello() {
```

```
        return "Hello, Spring Boot 3!";
    }
}
```

Step 5: Run Your Application

Open your terminal in the project's root directory.

Run the application with Maven:

```
mvn spring-boot:run
```

Open a web browser and navigate to

`http://localhost:8080/hello.`

You should see the message:

```
Hello, Spring Boot 3!
```

Step 6: Explore Application Configuration

Open `application.properties` in `src/main/resources`

and add configurations as needed, such as port

changes:

```
server.port=8081
```

By completing this section, you've successfully created

your first Spring Boot application. In the upcoming

chapters, we'll dive deeper into building RESTful APIs,

integrating databases, and connecting the backend with a React frontend.

Key Takeaways

Introduction to Spring Framework: Understanding the foundational components and architecture of the Spring Framework.

Spring Boot 3 Enhancements: Awareness of the latest features and improvements in Spring Boot 3, enabling more efficient and robust application development.

Building a Spring Boot Application: Practical knowledge of setting up, configuring, and deploying a basic Spring Boot application, including essential tools and dependencies.

Journal Exercises

1. **Reflection on Spring Framework:** Describe your current understanding of the Spring Framework. How

do you anticipate Spring Boot will streamline your development workflow?

_____

_____

_____

_____

_____

_____

_____

_____

_____

_____

2. **Exploring Spring Boot 3:** List and explain three new features introduced in Spring Boot 3. How can each feature be leveraged in modern applications?

_____

_____

_____

_____

_____

_____

_____

_____

_____

_____

_____

3. **First Application Journey:** Document the step-by-step process you followed to build your first Spring Boot application. What were the key challenges, and how did you address them?

_____

_____

_____

_____

_____

_____

_____

_____

_____

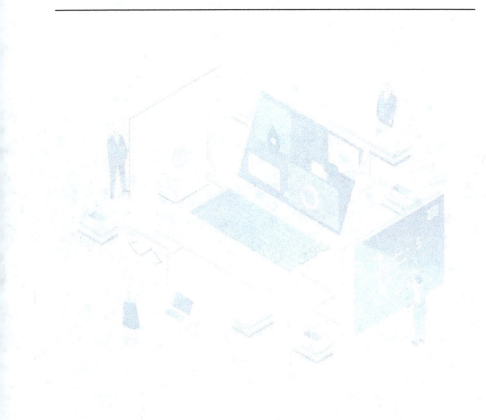

NOTES

CHAPTER 2

BUILDING RESTful APIs

RESTful APIs (Representational State Transfer APIs) are a cornerstone of modern web applications, allowing seamless communication between the backend and frontend. In this chapter, we'll explore the principles of REST, how to build RESTful endpoints with Spring Boot, handle HTTP methods effectively, and test APIs using Postman.

Understanding REST Principles

REST is an architectural style for designing networked applications. It relies on a stateless, client-server communication model, typically leveraging HTTP for data exchange.

Key Principles of REST

1. **Stateless Communication**

- Each API request from the client must contain all the information necessary for the server to process it. No client context is stored on the server between requests.

2. Client-Server Separation

- The client (frontend) and server (backend) are separate entities that communicate over RESTful APIs, ensuring modularity and scalability.

3. Resource-Based Architecture

- REST treats every object in the system as a resource (e.g., a user, product, or order). Each resource is identified by a unique URI (Uniform Resource Identifier).
- Example: `/users/1`

  refers to a specific user resource with ID 1.

4. Use of Standard HTTP Methods

- RESTful APIs use HTTP methods to perform operations on resources:
- **GET:** Retrieve a resource.
- **POST:** Create a new resource.
- **PUT:** Update an existing resource.
- **DELETE:** Remove a resource.

5. **Representation of Resources**
   - Resources can be represented in multiple formats, such as JSON or XML, with JSON being the most common.
6. **Stateless Responses with Hypermedia**
   - Responses should include all necessary details about the resource and possible actions, often following HATEOAS (Hypermedia as the Engine of Application State).

Creating REST Endpoints with Spring Boot

Step 1: Set Up the Project

- Use Spring Initializr to create a Spring Boot project with the following dependencies:
- **Spring Web**
- **Spring Boot DevTools** (optional, for auto-restarting the app)

Step 2: Define a Resource (Entity)

Let's consider an example resource: `Product`. Create a new class in the `com.example.demo` package:

```java
package com.example.demo;
public class Product {
    private Long id;
    private String name;
    private double price;

    // Constructors, Getters, and Setters
    public Product(Long id, String name, double price) {
        this.id = id;
        this.name = name;
        this.price = price;
    }
}
```

```java
public Long getId() {
    return id;
}

public void setId(Long id) {
    this.id = id;
}

public String getName() {
    return name;
}

public void setName(String name) {
    this.name = name;
}

public double getPrice() {
    return price;
}

public void setPrice(double price) {
    this.price = price;
}
}
```

Step 3: Create a REST Controller

A REST controller handles incoming HTTP requests and maps them to appropriate methods.

```java
package com.example.demo;

import org.springframework.web.bind.annotation.*;
import java.util.ArrayList;
import java.util.List;

@RestController
@RequestMapping("/products")
public class ProductController {
    private    List<Product>    productList    =    new
ArrayList<>();

    @GetMapping
    public List<Product> getAllProducts() {
        return productList;
    }

    @PostMapping
```

```java
    public      Product       createProduct(@RequestBody
Product product) {
        productList.add(product);
        return product;
    }


    @GetMapping("/{id}")
    public Product getProductById(@PathVariable Long
id) {
        return productList.stream()
            .filter(product                         ->
product.getId().equals(id))
            .findFirst()
            .orElseThrow(()              ->         new
RuntimeException("Product not found"));
    }


    @PutMapping("/{id}")
    public Product updateProduct(@PathVariable Long
id, @RequestBody Product updatedProduct) {
        Product product = getProductById(id);
        product.setName(updatedProduct.getName());
        product.setPrice(updatedProduct.getPrice());
        return product;
    }
```

```
@DeleteMapping("/{id}")
public String deleteProduct(@PathVariable Long
id) {
    Product product = getProductById(id);
    productList.remove(product);
    return "Product deleted successfully!";
}
}
```

Handling HTTP Methods: GET, POST, PUT, DELETE

1. GET Method

Retrieves data from the server.

Example: /products returns all products.

Implementation:

```
@GetMapping
public List<Product> getAllProducts() {
    return productList;
}
```

2. POST Method

Adds a new resource to the server.

Example: /products creates a new product.

Implementation:

```
@PostMapping
public Product createProduct(@RequestBody Product
product) {
    productList.add(product);
    return product;
}
```

3. PUT Method

Updates an existing resource.

Example: /products/{id} updates the product with the given ID.

Implementation:

```
@PutMapping("/{id}")
public Product updateProduct(@PathVariable Long id,
@RequestBody Product updatedProduct) {
    Product product = getProductById(id);
    product.setName(updatedProduct.getName());
    product.setPrice(updatedProduct.getPrice());
    return product;
}
```

4. DELETE Method

Removes a resource from the server.

Example: `/products/{id}` deletes the product with the given ID.

Implementation:

```
@DeleteMapping("/{id}")
public String deleteProduct(@PathVariable Long id) {
    Product product = getProductById(id);
    productList.remove(product);
    return "Product deleted successfully!";
}
```

Using Postman to Test APIs

Postman is a popular tool for testing and debugging RESTful APIs.

Step 1: Install Postman

Download and install Postman from [Postman's website](#).

Step 2: Test API Endpoints

GET Request

- URL: `http://localhost:8080/products`
- Method: GET
- Verify the response shows a list of products (initially empty).

POST Request

- URL: `http://localhost:8080/products`
- Method: POST
- Body (JSON):

```
{
    "id": 1,
    "name": "Laptop",
    "price": 1500.0
}
```

- Verify that the new product is added.

PUT Request

- URL: `http://localhost:8080/products/1`
- Method: PUT
- Body (JSON):

```
{
    "name": "Updated Laptop",
    "price": 1600.0
}
```

- Verify the product is updated.

DELETE Request

- URL: `http://localhost:8080/products/1`
- Method: DELETE
- Verify the product is removed.

With these fundamentals, you now have a fully functional RESTful API for managing resources. In the next chapter, we'll explore integrating this backend with a frontend application using React.

Key Takeaways

REST Principles: Comprehensive understanding of REST architectural style, including statelessness, client-server separation, and uniform interface.

Creating REST Endpoints: Practical skills in designing and implementing RESTful endpoints using Spring Boot, adhering to best practices.

API Testing with Postman: Proficiency in using Postman for testing and validating API endpoints, ensuring they meet functional requirements.

Journal Exercises

1. **Understanding REST Principles:** Explain the core principles of REST. How do these principles influence API design?

_____

_____

_____

2. _____

_____

_____

_____

_____

_____

3. **RESTful vs. Other API Styles:** Compare REST with at least two other API architectural styles. What are the advantages and disadvantages of each?

_____

_____

_____

_____

_____

_____

_____

_____

_____

_____

_____

_____

3. **API Testing with Postman:** Create a simple REST endpoint using Spring Boot and test it using Postman. Document any issues encountered during testing and how you resolved them.

_____

_____

NOTES

CHAPTER 3

DATA PERSISTENCE AND JPA

In any modern web application, data persistence is a fundamental requirement. **Spring Data JPA** simplifies database access and management, providing powerful abstractions to interact with relational databases. This chapter explores integrating Spring Data JPA, working with popular databases like H2, MySQL, and PostgreSQL, building repositories, performing CRUD operations, and writing custom queries.

Integrating Spring Data JPA

What is Spring Data JPA?

Spring Data JPA is a part of the larger Spring Data project. It simplifies working with Java Persistence API (JPA) by offering repository abstractions and reducing boilerplate code.

Why Use Spring Data JPA?

Automates common database operations (CRUD).

Provides an abstraction layer over JPA implementations (e.g., Hibernate).

Reduces boilerplate with features like derived query methods and custom repositories.

Steps to Integrate Spring Data JPA

1. **Add Dependencies**

   Include the following dependencies in your `pom.xml` file for Maven:

```xml
<dependencies>
    <dependency>
        <groupId>org.springframework.boot</groupId>
        <artifactId>spring-boot-starter-data-
jpa</artifactId>
    </dependency>
    <dependency>
        <groupId>com.h2database</groupId>
        <artifactId>h2</artifactId>
        <scope>runtime</scope>
    </dependency>
```

```
</dependencies>
```

2. Configure Database Properties

In `application.properties` or `application.yml`, define the

database configuration:

```
spring.datasource.url=jdbc:h2:mem:testdb
spring.datasource.username=sa
spring.datasource.password=
spring.datasource.driver-class-name=org.h2.Driver
spring.jpa.database-
platform=org.hibernate.dialect.H2Dialect
```

3. Annotate Your Entity Classes

Mark your classes with `@Entity` and map them to

database tables:

```java
import jakarta.persistence.Entity;
import jakarta.persistence.GeneratedValue;
import jakarta.persistence.GenerationType;
import jakarta.persistence.Id;

@Entity
public class Product {
    @Id
```

```
    @GeneratedValue(strategy=
GenerationType.IDENTITY)
    private Long id;
    private String name;
    private double price;

    // Getters and Setters
}
```

Working with H2, MySQL, and PostgreSQL

1. H2 Database

H2 is an in-memory database ideal for testing and development.

- No additional installation is required.
- The database is automatically created and destroyed with the application lifecycle.

Access the H2 console by enabling it in `application.properties`:

```
spring.h2.console.enabled=true
spring.h2.console.path=/h2-console
```

Visit `http://localhost:8080/h2-console` to explore the database.

2. MySQL

To use MySQL, include its dependency:

```xml
<dependency>
    <groupId>mysql</groupId>
    <artifactId>mysql-connector-java</artifactId>
    <scope>runtime</scope>
</dependency>
```

Update `application.properties`:

```properties
spring.datasource.url=jdbc:mysql://localhost:3306/mydatabase
spring.datasource.username=root
spring.datasource.password=password
spring.jpa.database-platform=org.hibernate.dialect.MySQLDialect
```

3. PostgreSQL

To use PostgreSQL, include its dependency:

```xml
<dependency>
```

```
    <groupId>org.postgresql</groupId>
    <artifactId>postgresql</artifactId>
    <scope>runtime</scope>
</dependency>
```

Update **application.properties**:

```
spring.datasource.url=jdbc:postgresql://localhost:54
32/mydatabase
spring.datasource.username=postgres
spring.datasource.password=password
spring.jpa.database-
platform=org.hibernate.dialect.PostgreSQLDialect
```

Building Repositories and CRUD Operations

Defining a Repository

Spring Data JPA uses the repository pattern to abstract database interactions. Create an interface extending **JpaRepository** to gain access to CRUD methods.

```
import
org.springframework.data.jpa.repository.JpaRepositor
y;
```

```java
public     interface     ProductRepository     extends
JpaRepository<Product, Long> {

}
```

Performing CRUD Operations

Here's how to use `JpaRepository` methods for CRUD
operations:

Create

```java
Product product = new Product();
product.setName("Laptop");
product.setPrice(1500.0);
productRepository.save(product);
```

Read

```java
// Find all products
List<Product>                products            =
productRepository.findAll();


// Find product by ID
Optional<Product>                product            =
productRepository.findById(1L);
```

Update

```java
Product                    existingProduct            =
productRepository.findById(1L).orElseThrow();
```

```
existingProduct.setPrice(1600.0);
productRepository.save(existingProduct);
```

Delete

```
productRepository.deleteById(1L);
```

Introduction to Query Methods and Custom Queries

1. Query Methods

Spring Data JPA allows you to define queries based on method names, using conventions like **findBy, countBy,** and **deleteBy.**

Examples:

```
// Find products by name
List<Product> findByName(String name);


// Find products with a price greater than a value
List<Product> findByPriceGreaterThan(double price);
```

2. Custom JPQL Queries

Use **@Query** annotation to define custom JPQL (Java Persistence Query Language) queries:

```java
import
org.springframework.data.jpa.repository.Query;
import
org.springframework.data.repository.query.Param;

public    interface    ProductRepository    extends
JpaRepository<Product, Long> {
    @Query("SELECT p FROM Product p WHERE p.price >
:price")
    List<Product>
findExpensiveProducts(@Param("price") double price);
}
```

3. Native SQL Queries

For raw SQL, use the `nativeQuery` flag:

```java
@Query(value = "SELECT * FROM product WHERE price >
:price", nativeQuery = true)
List<Product>
findExpensiveProductsNative(@Param("price")    double
price);
```

Summary

In this chapter, you've learned how to integrate Spring
Data JPA with popular databases, build repositories,

and perform CRUD operations. With the ability to write custom queries and leverage query methods, you now have the tools to interact with a database efficiently. In the next chapter, we'll explore connecting the backend to a React frontend to create a seamless full stack application.

Key Takeaways

Spring Data JPA Integration: Understanding how to incorporate Spring Data JPA for seamless data persistence in Spring Boot applications.

Database Selection: Insights into different relational databases (H2, MySQL, PostgreSQL) and their use cases.

Repositories and CRUD Operations: Ability to create repositories, perform CRUD operations, and utilize query methods and custom queries for data manipulation.

Journal Exercises

1. **Spring Data JPA Integration:** Describe the process of integrating Spring Data JPA into a Spring Boot application. What configurations are necessary?

   _____

   _____

   _____

   _____

_____

_____

_____

2. **Choosing a Database:** Compare H2, MySQL, and PostgreSQL. For what types of projects is each database best suited?

_____

_____

_____

_____

_____

_____

3. **CRUD Operations Practice:** Implement CRUD operations for a sample entity. Reflect on the

challenges faced while building repositories and performing these operations.

_____

_____

_____

_____

_____

_____

_____

NOTES

CHAPTER 4

ADVANCED BACKEND FEATURES

This chapter delves into critical backend features that elevate the quality, security, and maintainability of your application. These advanced concepts—authentication, authorization, secure APIs, robust error handling, and effective monitoring—are essential for building enterprise-grade web applications.

Spring Boot Security: Authentication and Authorization

Understanding Authentication and Authorization

Authentication

- Verifies the identity of a user or system.
- Example: Logging in with a username and password.

Authorization

- Determines what resources or actions an authenticated user can access.

- Example: Allowing only admins to modify user data.

Spring Security, part of the Spring ecosystem, is a powerful framework for managing both authentication and authorization.

Setting Up Spring Security

1. Add Dependencies

Include the following dependencies in your `pom.xml`:

```xml
<dependency>
    <groupId>org.springframework.boot</groupId>
    <artifactId>spring-boot-starter-security</artifactId>
</dependency>
```

2. Configure Basic Security

Spring Security enforces a default login form. You can configure it for custom authentication and authorization rules:

Security Configuration Class:

```java
import org.springframework.context.annotation.Bean;
```

```java
import
org.springframework.context.annotation.Configuration
;
import
org.springframework.security.config.annotation.web.b
uilders.HttpSecurity;
import
org.springframework.security.crypto.bcrypt.BCryptPas
swordEncoder;
import
org.springframework.security.crypto.password.Passwor
dEncoder;
import
org.springframework.security.web.SecurityFilterChain
;

@Configuration
public class SecurityConfig {

    @Bean
    public                          SecurityFilterChain
securityFilterChain(HttpSecurity    http)    throws
Exception {
        http
            .csrf().disable()
```

```
            .authorizeRequests()

.antMatchers("/admin/**").hasRole("ADMIN")

.antMatchers("/user/**").hasAnyRole("USER", "ADMIN")

.antMatchers("/public/**").permitAll()
                .and()
            .httpBasic();
        return http.build();
    }


    @Bean
    public PasswordEncoder passwordEncoder() {
        return new BCryptPasswordEncoder();

    }
}
```

Endpoints Protection:

/admin/** is accessible only to users with the ADMIN role.

/user/** is accessible to users with USER or ADMIN roles.

/public/** is open to all.

Implementing JWT for Secure APIs

JSON Web Tokens (JWT) are compact, self-contained tokens used for secure communication between parties. JWTs eliminate the need for maintaining session state on the server.

How JWT Works

A client logs in and provides valid credentials.

The server generates a JWT and returns it to the client.

The client includes the JWT in the `Authorization` header for subsequent requests.

The server verifies the token and grants access to protected resources.

Steps to Implement JWT

1. Add Dependencies

Add the following dependencies to your `pom.xml`:

```xml
<dependency>
    <groupId>io.jsonwebtoken</groupId>
    <artifactId>jjwt-api</artifactId>
```

```xml
        <version>0.11.5</version>
</dependency>
<dependency>
    <groupId>io.jsonwebtoken</groupId>
    <artifactId>jjwt-impl</artifactId>
    <version>0.11.5</version>
</dependency>
<dependency>
    <groupId>io.jsonwebtoken</groupId>
    <artifactId>jjwt-jackson</artifactId>
    <version>0.11.5</version>
</dependency>
```

2. Generate and Validate JWT

JWT Utility Class:

```java
import io.jsonwebtoken.Jwts;
import io.jsonwebtoken.SignatureAlgorithm;

import java.util.Date;

public class JwtUtil {
    private static final String SECRET_KEY =
"my_secret_key";
```

```java
    public String generateToken(String username) {
        return Jwts.builder()
            .setSubject(username)
            .setIssuedAt(new Date())
            .setExpiration(new
Date(System.currentTimeMillis() + 1000 * 60 * 60))
            .signWith(SignatureAlgorithm.HS256,
SECRET_KEY)
            .compact();
    }

    public boolean validateToken(String token) {
        try {

Jwts.parser().setSigningKey(SECRET_KEY).parseClaimsJ
ws(token);
            return true;
        } catch (Exception e) {
            return false;


    }

    }
```

} 3. Integrate JWT with Spring Security

Add JWT validation logic to your `SecurityConfig`.
Intercept requests using a filter to validate the JWT.

1. Exception Handling with @ControllerAdvice

Spring provides a global exception-handling mechanism with `@ControllerAdvice`.

Global Exception Handler:

```java
import org.springframework.http.HttpStatus;
import org.springframework.http.ResponseEntity;
import org.springframework.web.bind.annotation.ControllerAdvice;
import org.springframework.web.bind.annotation.ExceptionHandler;

@ControllerAdvice
public class GlobalExceptionHandler {



@ExceptionHandler(ResourceNotFoundException.class)
```

```java
    public                         ResponseEntity<String>
handleResourceNotFound(ResourceNotFoundException ex)
{
        return new ResponseEntity<>(ex.getMessage(),
HttpStatus.NOT_FOUND);
    }


    @ExceptionHandler(Exception.class)
    public                         ResponseEntity<String>
handleGenericException(Exception ex) {
        return   new   ResponseEntity<>("An   error
occurred:         "         +         ex.getMessage(),
HttpStatus.INTERNAL_SERVER_ERROR);
    }
}
```

Custom Exception:

```java
public   class   ResourceNotFoundException   extends
RuntimeException {
    public ResourceNotFoundException(String message)
{
        super(message);
    }
}
```

2. Validation with @Valid

Spring's validation framework simplifies input validation.

Example Entity with Validation:

```java
import jakarta.validation.constraints.NotBlank;
import jakarta.validation.constraints.Positive;

public class Product {
    @NotBlank(message = "Name is required")
    private String name;

    @Positive(message = "Price must be positive")
    private double price;
}
```

Controller Example:

```java
@PostMapping("/products")
public ResponseEntity<Product> createProduct(@Valid
@RequestBody Product product) {
    return ResponseEntity.ok(product);
}
```

Spring Boot Actuator provides endpoints for monitoring and managing applications.

1. Adding Actuator Dependency

Add this dependency to your `pom.xml`:

```xml
<dependency>
    <groupId>org.springframework.boot</groupId>
    <artifactId>spring-boot-starter-actuator</artifactId>
</dependency>
```

2. Enable Actuator Endpoints

Configure `application.properties` to expose Actuator endpoints:

```
management.endpoints.web.exposure.include=health,info
management.endpoint.health.show-details=always
```

3. Common Endpoints

`/actuator/health`: Application health status.

`/actuator/info`: Displays custom application info.

Adding Custom Info:

```java
import org.springframework.boot.actuate.info.Info;
import org.springframework.boot.actuate.info.InfoContributor;
import org.springframework.stereotype.Component;

@Component
public class CustomInfoContributor implements InfoContributor {
    @Override
    public void contribute(Info.Builder builder) {
        builder.withDetail("app", "Spring Boot Demo Application")
            .withDetail("version", "1.0.0");
    }
}
```

4. Logging

Configure logging in **application.properties**:

```
logging.level.org.springframework=INFO
logging.level.com.example=DEBUG
```

With these advanced features, your backend is now secure, reliable, and easy to monitor. In the next chapter, we'll focus on integrating this backend with a React-based frontend to build a complete full stack application.

Key Takeaways

Authentication and Authorization: In-depth understanding of securing applications using Spring Boot Security, differentiating between authentication and authorization mechanisms.

JWT Implementation: Knowledge of JSON Web Tokens (JWT) for securing APIs, including setup and integration within Spring Boot.

Exception Handling and Monitoring: Techniques for effective exception handling, validation, and utilizing Spring Boot Actuator for logging and monitoring application health.

Journal Exercises

1. **Spring Boot Security Fundamentals:** Explain the differences between authentication and authorization. How does Spring Boot facilitate each?

_____

_____

_____

_____

_____

_____

2. **Implementing JWT:** Outline the steps you took to implement JWT in your Spring Boot application. What security benefits does JWT provide?

_____

_____

_____

_____

_____

_____

_____

3. **Exception Handling Strategies:** Reflect on the importance of exception handling and validation in backend development. How did you implement these in your project?

_____

_____

_____

_____

_____

NOTES

PART 2

FRONTEND DEVELOPMENT WITH REACT

CHAPTER 5

GETTING STARTED WITH REACT

React is one of the most popular JavaScript libraries for building dynamic, fast, and user-friendly web applications. This chapter introduces the fundamentals of React, walks you through setting up a React project, and demonstrates how to create a simple React component.

React Basics:

React is built on three core concepts: **Components**, **Props**, and **State**. Understanding these will form the foundation for mastering React.

1. Components

Components are the building blocks of a React application.

Each component is a JavaScript function or class that returns React elements (essentially HTML-like code).

Components can be reused, making development efficient and scalable.

Types of Components

Functional Components

Simple JavaScript functions that return JSX.

Example:

```
function Greeting() {
    return <h1>Hello, React!</h1>;
}
```

Class Components (less commonly used in modern React)

ES6 classes with lifecycle methods.

2. **Props (Properties)**

Props are a way to pass data from parent to child components.

Props are **read-only** and cannot be modified by the child component.

Example:

```
function Welcome(props) {
    return <h1>Welcome, {props.name}!</h1>;
}


// Usage
<Welcome name="John" />
```

3. State

State is a way to manage dynamic data within a component.

Unlike props, state is **mutable** and can be updated using the `useState` hook (in functional components).

Example of State Management with useState

```
import React, { useState } from 'react';


function Counter() {
    const [count, setCount] = useState(0);


    return (
        <div>
            <p>Count: {count}</p>
```

```
        <button onClick={() => setCount(count +
1)}>Increase</button>
        </div>
    );
}
```

Setting Up a React Project with Vite or Create-React-App

To start a React project, you can use **Create-React-App (CRA)** or **Vite**. While CRA is widely known, Vite is a modern alternative with faster builds and development performance.

1. Using Create-React-App (CRA)

Step 1: Install Node.js

Ensure Node.js is installed. Verify with:

```
node -v
npm -v
```

Step 2: Create a React Project

Run the following command:

```
npx create-react-app my-app
```

Step 3: Navigate to the Project Directory

```
cd my-app
```

Step 4: Start the Development Server

```
npm start
```

The app will run at `http://localhost:3000`.

2. Using Vite

Vite offers faster development and builds for modern projects.

Step 1: Install Node.js

Ensure Node.js is installed as above.

Step 2: Create a React Project with Vite

Run the following command:

```
npm create vite@latest my-app --template react
```

Step 3: Navigate to the Project Directory

```
cd my-app
```

Step 4: Install Dependencies

```
npm install
```

Step 5: Start the Development Server

```
npm run dev
```

The app will run at a URL similar to `http://localhost:5173`.

Building a Simple React Component

Step 1: Set Up the Component Structure

Inside the `src` folder, create a new file named `Greeting.js`.

Write the following code:

```
import React from 'react';

function Greeting({ name }) {
    return <h1>Hello, {name}!</h1>;
}

export default Greeting;
```

Explanation:

- `Greeting` is a functional component that accepts a `name` prop and displays a personalized message.

Step 2: Use the Component in App.js

Open `src/App.js`.

Modify the file as follows:

```javascript
import React from 'react';
import Greeting from './Greeting';

function App() {
    return (
        <div>
            <Greeting name="John" />
            <Greeting name="Jane" />
        </div>
    );
}

export default App;
```

Step 3: Run the Application

Start the development server using `npm start` (for CRA) or `npm run dev` (for Vite).

Open your browser and visit the URL (e.g., `http://localhost:3000` or `http://localhost:5173`).

You should see:

```
Hello, John!
Hello, Jane!
```

Summary

In this chapter, we've covered React fundamentals: components, props, and state. You also learned how to set up a React project using Create-React-App or Vite and create a simple component. In the next chapter, we'll dive deeper into state management and explore tools like Context API and Redux for building complex applications.

Key Takeaways

React Basics: Mastery of core React concepts including components, props, and state management.

Project Setup: Ability to set up React projects using popular tools like Vite or Create-React-App, understanding the pros and cons of each.

Component Development: Practical experience in building and rendering React components, laying the foundation for more complex UI development.

Journal Exercises

1. **React Fundamentals:** Define components, props, and state in React. How do they interact within a React application?

_____

_____

_____

_____

_____

_____

2. **Project Setup Comparison:** Set up a React project using both Vite and Create-React-App. Compare the experiences and note any differences in performance or configuration.

_____

_____

_____

_____

_____

_____

3. **Building Components:** Create a simple React component and document the process. What did you learn about component lifecycle and state management?

NOTES

CHAPTER 6

STATE MANAGEMENT

State management is at the heart of building dynamic and interactive React applications. It allows developers to handle changes to data and synchronize the user interface (UI) with application logic. This chapter introduces React Hooks (`useState` and `useEffect`), explores the Context API for managing state across components, and provides an introduction to Redux for handling complex application state.

Understanding React Hooks (`useState`, `useEffect`)

React Hooks provide a way to use state and lifecycle methods in functional components, eliminating the need for class components.

1. The `useState` Hook

The `useState` Hook allows functional components to manage local state.

Syntax

```
const [state, setState] = useState(initialValue);
```

state: The current state value.

setState: A function to update the state.

initialValue: The initial state value.

Example: Counter Component

```jsx
import React, { useState } from 'react';

function Counter() {
    const [count, setCount] = useState(0);

    return (
        <div>
            <p>Current Count: {count}</p>
            <button onClick={() => setCount(count +
1)}>Increment</button>
            <button onClick={() => setCount(count -
1)}>Decrement</button>
        </div>
    );
}
```

```
export default Counter;
```

When the buttons are clicked, the `setCount` function updates the `count` state, and the UI re-renders.

2. The `useEffect` Hook

The `useEffect` Hook is used to perform side effects, such as fetching data, updating the DOM, or setting up subscriptions.

Syntax

```
useEffect(() => {
    // Side effect logic here
    return () => {
        // Cleanup logic here (optional)
    };
}, [dependencies]);
```

Dependencies: A list of variables that, when changed, will trigger the effect. Leaving this list empty (`[]`) means the effect runs only once.

Example: Fetching Data with `useEffect`

```javascript
import React, { useState, useEffect } from 'react';

function DataFetcher() {
    const [data, setData] = useState([]);
    const [loading, setLoading] = useState(true);

    useEffect(() => {

fetch('https://jsonplaceholder.typicode.com/posts')
            .then((response) => response.json())
            .then((json) => {
                setData(json);
                setLoading(false);
            });
    }, []);

    if (loading) {
        return <p>Loading...</p>;
    }

    return (
        <ul>
            {data.slice(0, 5).map((item) => (
                <li key={item.id}>{item.title}</li>
```

```
              )))
        </ul>
    );

}


export default DataFetcher;
```

The `useEffect` hook fetches data when the component mounts and updates the state with the fetched data.

The Context API provides a way to share state across components without passing props manually through every level of the component tree. It is ideal for medium-sized applications or when global state sharing is required.

1. Creating a Context

Create a new context using `React.createContext()`.

Example: User Context

```
import React, { createContext, useState } from
'react';

export const UserContext = createContext();

export function UserProvider({ children }) {
    const [user, setUser] = useState({ name: 'John
Doe', age: 30 });

    return (
        <UserContext.Provider value={{ user, setUser
}}>
            {children}
        </UserContext.Provider>
    );
}
```

The **UserProvider** component wraps the app and provides the user state to all child components.

2. Consuming Context

Use the **useContext** Hook to access context values.

Example: Accessing User Context

```
import React, { useContext } from 'react';
```

```
import { UserContext } from './UserContext';

function UserProfile() {
    const { user } = useContext(UserContext);

    return (
        <div>
            <h1>{user.name}</h1>
            <p>Age: {user.age}</p>
        </div>
    );
}

export default UserProfile;
```

3. Integrating Context in the Application

Wrap the root component with the context provider in

`index.js` or `App.js`:

```
import React from 'react';
import ReactDOM from 'react-dom';
import { UserProvider } from './UserContext';
import App from './App';

ReactDOM.render(
```

```
<UserProvider>
    <App />
</UserProvider>,
document.getElementById('root')
);
```

Introduction to Redux for Complex Applications

1. What is Redux?

Redux is a state management library for JavaScript applications. It is particularly useful for managing complex state that spans across multiple components. Redux operates on three core principles:

Single Source of Truth:

The state of the application is stored in a single object called the "store."

State is Read-Only:

The only way to change the state is through "actions."

Changes are Made with Pure Functions:

Reducers, which are pure functions, specify how the state changes in response to actions.

2. Setting Up Redux in a React Application

Step 1: Add Dependencies

Install Redux and React-Redux:

```
npm install redux react-redux
```

Step 2: Create a Redux Store

```
import { createStore } from 'redux';

// Initial State
const initialState = {
    counter: 0,
};

// Reducer
function counterReducer(state = initialState, action)
{
    switch (action.type) {
        case 'INCREMENT':
            return { ...state, counter: state.counter
+ 1 };
        case 'DECREMENT':
            return { ...state, counter: state.counter
- 1 };
```

```
        default:
            return state;
    }
}


// Store
const store = createStore(counterReducer);


export default store;
```

Step 3: Provide the Store to React

Use the **Provider** component to pass the store to the application.

```
import React from 'react';
import ReactDOM from 'react-dom';
import { Provider } from 'react-redux';
import store from './store';
import App from './App';


ReactDOM.render(
    <Provider store={store}>
        <App />
    </Provider>,
    document.getElementById('root')
```

```
);
```

Step 4: Access the State and Dispatch Actions

Use **useSelector** to access the state and **useDispatch** to dispatch actions.

Counter Component:

```jsx
import React from 'react';
import { useSelector, useDispatch } from 'react-redux';

function Counter() {
    const counter = useSelector((state) =>
state.counter);
    const dispatch = useDispatch();

    return (
        <div>
            <h1>Counter: {counter}</h1>
            <button onClick={() => dispatch({ type:
'INCREMENT' })}>Increment</button>
            <button onClick={() => dispatch({ type:
'DECREMENT' })}>Decrement</button>
        </div>
```

```
    );
}

export default Counter;
```

Context API vs. Redux

Use **Context API** for simpler, localized state management.

Choose **Redux** for complex applications requiring centralized state management and predictable updates.

In this chapter, you learned the fundamentals of state management in React, explored Hooks like `useState` and `useEffect`, implemented global state sharing with the Context API, and set up Redux for managing complex application state. These tools empower you to manage state efficiently and build dynamic, feature-rich applications.

Key Takeaways

React Hooks: Comprehensive understanding of `useState` and `useEffect` hooks for managing state and side effects in functional components.

State Management Solutions: Insight into the Context API and Redux, including their use cases, advantages, and limitations.

Advanced State Handling: Ability to implement complex state management strategies using Redux for larger and more intricate applications.

Journal Exercises

1. **React Hooks Exploration:** Experiment with `useState` and `useEffect` hooks in a React application. How do they simplify state management and side effects?

_____

_____

_____

_____

_____

_____

_____

2. **Context API vs. Redux:** Compare and contrast the Context API and Redux for state management. In what scenarios would you prefer one over the other?

_____

_____

_____

_____

_____

_____

_____

3. **Implementing Redux:** Set up Redux in a small React project. Document the steps and any challenges faced during the integration.

NOTE

CHAPTER 7

REACT ROUTER AND NAVIGATION

Routing is a critical feature for building single-page applications (SPAs) in React. React Router, a powerful library, provides dynamic routing capabilities that allow developers to define routes, manage navigation, and create a seamless user experience. This chapter covers setting up React Router, creating routes (including nested routes), and managing navigation and redirects.

Setting Up React Router

React Router enables navigation between different views or pages in a React application without refreshing the page.

1. Install React Router

To use React Router, add it to your project:

```
npm install react-router-dom
```

2. Understand Core Concepts

Router: The component that enables routing. Common routers include `BrowserRouter` (for web apps) and `HashRouter`.

Route: Defines the path and the component to render.

Link: A React component that creates navigation links.

Switch/Routes: Ensures only the first matching route is rendered (in older versions, `Switch` was used; now `Routes` is used in React Router v6+).

3. Basic Setup

Modify `src/index.js` to wrap your app in a router:

```
import React from 'react';
import ReactDOM from 'react-dom';
import { BrowserRouter } from 'react-router-dom';
import App from './App';

ReactDOM.render(
    <BrowserRouter>
        <App />
    </BrowserRouter>,
    document.getElementById('root')
```

```
);
```

Creating Routes and Nested Routes

1. Defining Routes

Routes map URL paths to components. Update src/App.js to define some routes:

```
import React from 'react';
import { Routes, Route } from 'react-router-dom';
import Home from './Home';
import About from './About';
import Contact from './Contact';

function App() {
    return (
        <Routes>
            <Route path="/" element={<Home />} />
            <Route path="/about" element={<About />}
/>
            <Route path="/contact" element={<Contact
/>} />
        </Routes>
    );
```

```
}

export default App;
```

Explanation:

The `path` prop specifies the URL.

The `element` prop specifies the component to render.

2. Creating Components

Create basic components for the routes:

Home.js

```
import React from 'react';

function Home() {
    return <h1>Welcome to the Home Page</h1>;
}

export default Home;
```

About.js

```
import React from 'react';

function About() {
    return <h1>About Us</h1>;
```

```
}

export default About;
```

Contact.js

```
import React from 'react';

function Contact() {
    return <h1>Contact Us</h1>;
}

export default Contact;
```

3. Nested Routes

React Router supports nested routes for creating hierarchical navigation.

Update `App.js` to include nested routes:

```
import React from 'react';
import { Routes, Route } from 'react-router-dom';
import Home from './Home';
import About from './About';
import Contact from './Contact';
import Team from './Team';
```

```
import Mission from './Mission';

function App() {
    return (
        <Routes>
            <Route path="/" element={<Home />} />
            <Route path="/about" element={<About
/>}>
                <Route path="team" element={<Team
/>} />
                <Route path="mission"
element={<Mission />} />
            </Route>
            <Route path="/contact" element={<Contact
/>} />
        </Routes>
    );
}

export default App;
```

Nested Components (Team.js, Mission.js):
Team.js

```
import React from 'react';

function Team() {
    return <h2>Our Team</h2>;
}

export default Team;
```

Mission.js

```
import React from 'react';

function Mission() {
    return <h2>Our Mission</h2>;
}

export default Mission;
```

About.js with Outlet:

For nested routes, use `Outlet` to render child routes:

```
import React from 'react';
import { Outlet, Link } from 'react-router-dom';

function About() {
    return (
        <div>
```

```
        <h1>About Us</h1>
        <nav>
            <Link to="team">Our Team</Link> |
<Link to="mission">Our Mission</Link>
        </nav>
        <Outlet />
    </div>
  );
}


export default About;
```

Managing Navigation and Redirects

1. Navigation with `Link`

The `Link` component creates navigation links without reloading the page.

Example Navigation Bar:

```
import React from 'react';
import { Link } from 'react-router-dom';


function Navbar() {
    return (
```

```
        <nav>
            <Link to="/">Home</Link> |
            <Link to="/about">About</Link> |
            <Link to="/contact">Contact</Link>
        </nav>
    );
}


export default Navbar;
```

Integrate this **Navbar** in **App.js**:

```
function App() {
    return (
        <div>
            <Navbar />
            <Routes>
                <Route path="/" element={<Home />} />
                <Route path="/about" element={<About
/>} />
                <Route                  path="/contact"
element={<Contact />} />
            </Routes>
        </div>
    );
```

2. Programmatic Navigation with useNavigate

The useNavigate Hook allows programmatic navigation, useful for redirecting users after an action.

Example:

```
import React from 'react';
import { useNavigate } from 'react-router-dom';

function Login() {
    const navigate = useNavigate();

    const handleLogin = () => {
        // Perform login logic here
        navigate('/dashboard');
    };

    return (
        <div>
            <h1>Login Page</h1>
            <button
onClick={handleLogin}>Login</button>
        </div>
    );
```

```
}

export default Login;
```

3. Redirects

Redirects can be achieved using programmatic navigation or by defining default routes.

Example:

Redirect from / to /**home**:

```
import React from 'react';
import { Routes, Route, Navigate } from 'react-
router-dom';

function App() {
    return (
        <Routes>
            <Route     path="/"     element={<Navigate
to="/home" />} />
            <Route path="/home" element={<Home />} />
            <Route path="/about" element={<About />}
/>
            <Route path="/contact" element={<Contact
/>} />
```

```
        </Routes>
    );
}


export default App;
```

Best Practices for React Router

- Organize routes hierarchically to match your app's structure.

- Use `useNavigate` for dynamic and conditional navigation.

- Keep route definitions in a centralized file for maintainability.

- Use nested routes for related views to simplify your routing logic.

- Test all routes to ensure navigation works seamlessly.

React Router simplifies navigation and routing in React applications. In this chapter, you've learned to set up

React Router, define routes, implement nested routing, and manage navigation and redirects. These skills are essential for creating seamless user experiences in modern single-page applications.

Key Takeaways

React Router Integration: Proficiency in setting up and configuring React Router for managing client-side routing in React applications.

Nested Routing: Ability to create and manage nested routes, enhancing the structural organization of the application.

Navigation Techniques: Skills in managing navigation flows, including redirects and conditional rendering based on application state.

Journal Exercises

1. **Setting Up React Router:** Implement React Router in a sample project. How does routing enhance user experience in single-page applications?

_____

_____

_____

_____

_____

_____

2. **Nested Routes Implementation:** Create nested routes within your application. What challenges did you face, and how did you resolve them?

_____

_____

_____

_____

_____

_____

_____

3. **Navigation Management:** Experiment with navigation and redirects. How can you manage user navigation effectively to maintain application state?

_____

_____

_____

_____

_____

CHAPTER 8

STYLING AND UI DESIGN

Styling and user interface (UI) design are essential aspects of creating modern, visually appealing, and user-friendly web applications. In this chapter, we will explore methods to style React applications using **CSS Modules** and **Styled-Components**, leverage popular UI libraries like **Bootstrap** and **Material-UI**, and implement strategies for building **responsive and accessible UIs**.

Styling with CSS Modules and Styled-Components

1. CSS Modules

CSS Modules provide a way to scope styles to a specific component, avoiding global naming conflicts.

Setting Up CSS Modules

Create a CSS Module File:

Save the file with the `.module.css` extension. For example:

`Button`**`.module.css.`**

```css
/* Button.module.css */
.primary {
    background-color: #007bff;
    color: white;
    padding: 10px 20px;
    border: none;
    border-radius: 4px;
    cursor: pointer;
}

.secondary {
    background-color: #6c757d;
    color: white;
    padding: 10px 20px;
    border: none;
    border-radius: 4px;
    cursor: pointer;
}
```

Import and Use the CSS Module in a Component:

```javascript
import React from 'react';
import styles from './Button.module.css';


function Button({ type, label }) {
    return (
```

```
        <button className={styles[type]}>
            {label}
        </button>
    );
}
export default Button;
```

Pass **type** as **primary** or **secondary** to dynamically apply styles.

2. Styled-Components

Styled-Components is a library for writing CSS-in-JS, allowing you to define component-specific styles directly within JavaScript.

Installing Styled-Components

```
npm install styled-components
```

Defining Styled Components

Example: Button Component

```
import React from 'react';
import styled from 'styled-components';
```

```
const StyledButton = styled.button`
    padding: 10px 20px;
    border: none;
    border-radius: 4px;
    color: white;
    cursor: pointer;

    background-color: ${(props) =>
        props.type === 'primary' ? '#007bff' :
'#6c757d'};

    &:hover {
        opacity: 0.9;
    }
`;


function Button({ type, label }) {
    return                              <StyledButton
type={type}>{label}</StyledButton>;
}

export default Button;
```

Advantages of Styled-Components:

- CSS is scoped to components.
- Allows dynamic styling with props.
- Enables easier maintenance for component-based designs.

Using Libraries Like Bootstrap and Material-UI

1. Bootstrap

Bootstrap is a popular CSS framework for building responsive and mobile-first UIs.

Installing Bootstrap

Install Bootstrap using **npm**:

```
npm install bootstrap
```

Import Bootstrap in your **index.js** file:

```
import 'bootstrap/dist/css/bootstrap.min.css';
```

Using Bootstrap Classes

Bootstrap provides pre-defined classes for layout and components.

Example: Button Component

```
import React from 'react';
```

```
function BootstrapButton({ type, label }) {
    const className = type === 'primary' ? 'btn btn-
primary' : 'btn btn-secondary';
    return                                    <button
className={className}>{label}</button>;
}

export default BootstrapButton;
```

Using Bootstrap Grid System

The grid system allows for responsive layout design.

```
<div className="container">
    <div className="row">
        <div className="col-md-6">Column 1</div>
        <div className="col-md-6">Column 2</div>
    </div>
</div>
```

2. Material-UI (MUI)

Material-UI provides React components implementing Google's Material Design.

Installing Material-UI

Install the MUI library and its icons:

```
npm      install      @mui/material      @emotion/react
@emotion/styled @mui/icons-material
```

Using Material-UI Components

Example: Button Component

```
import React from 'react';
import Button from '@mui/material/Button';

function MUIButton({ type, label }) {
    return <Button variant={type}>{label}</Button>;
}

export default MUIButton;
```

Use **variant="contained"** for a filled button or **variant="outlined"** for an outlined one.

Using MUI Grid for Layout

```
import React from 'react';
import { Grid } from '@mui/material';

function Layout() {
    return (
        <Grid container spacing={2}>
```

```
            <Grid item xs={6}>Column 1</Grid>
            <Grid item xs={6}>Column 2</Grid>
        </Grid>
    );
}


export default Layout;
```

Creating Responsive and Accessible UIs

1. Responsive Design

Using Media Queries

Write media queries in CSS or Styled-Components to handle different screen sizes.

```css
/* Example in CSS */
@media (max-width: 768px) {
    .container {
        flex-direction: column;
    }
}
```

Responsive Design with Frameworks

Bootstrap: Use classes like `col-md-6, col-sm-12` to define responsive grids.

Material-UI: Use the `Grid` component with breakpoints like `xs, sm, md`.

Use Semantic HTML

Use proper tags like `<header>, <nav>, <main>`, and `<footer>` for better accessibility.

Provide ARIA Attributes

Add ARIA attributes for screen readers.

```
<button aria-label="Submit form">Submit</button>
```

Keyboard Navigation

Ensure all interactive elements (buttons, links, inputs) are keyboard accessible.

Color Contrast

Follow WCAG (Web Content Accessibility Guidelines) to ensure sufficient contrast between text and background colors.

- Use tools like Contrast Checker.

Best Practices for Styling and UI Design

1. Use a consistent design system across your application.
2. Leverage reusable components for common UI elements.
3. Optimize performance by loading only necessary CSS or JavaScript for UI libraries.
4. Always test for responsiveness and accessibility using tools like Lighthouse or Axe.

In this chapter, you've learned various ways to style React applications, including using CSS Modules, Styled-Components, and popular UI libraries like Bootstrap and Material-UI. You've also explored strategies for building responsive and accessible UIs, ensuring a superior user experience for all users.

Key Takeaways

Styling Techniques: Knowledge of various styling methods in React, including CSS Modules and Styled-Components, and their appropriate use cases.

UI Libraries Utilization: Ability to integrate and use UI libraries like Bootstrap and Material-UI to accelerate development and ensure consistency.

Responsive and Accessible Design: Understanding of responsive design principles and accessibility standards to create user-friendly and inclusive interfaces.

Journal Exercises

1. **CSS Modules vs. Styled-Components:** Implement styling using both CSS Modules and Styled-Components. Compare their approaches and effectiveness.

---

2. **Responsive Design Practice:** Design a responsive UI using Bootstrap or Material-UI. What considerations

did you make to ensure accessibility and responsiveness?

_____

_____

_____

_____

_____

_____

_____

3. **UI Design Best Practices:** Reflect on the best practices for UI design you applied in your project. How did they improve the user experience?

_____

_____

_____

_____

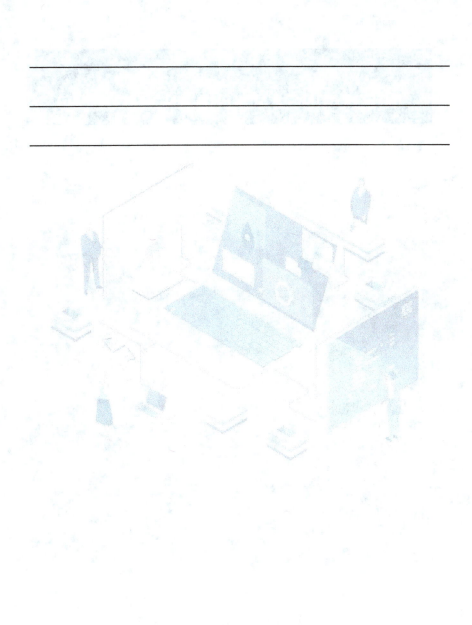

PART 3

INTEGRATING BACKEND AND FRONTEND

CHAPTER 9

CONNECTING REACT AND SPRING BOOT

Connecting the frontend (React) with the backend (Spring Boot) is a critical step in building full stack applications. This chapter covers key concepts and techniques for seamless integration, including configuring CORS in Spring Boot, fetching data using Axios or Fetch API, and sending form data to the backend while handling responses effectively.

Understanding CORS and Configuring it in Spring Boot

1. What is CORS?

CORS (Cross-Origin Resource Sharing) is a security feature in web browsers that restricts how resources on a server are accessed by clients from different origins.

- **Origin**: Defined by the combination of protocol (HTTP/HTTPS), domain, and port (e.g., `http://localhost:3000`).

- React (typically on port 3000) accessing a Spring Boot backend (on port 8080) is considered a cross-origin request.

If CORS is not configured, the browser will block these requests for security reasons.

2. Configuring CORS in Spring Boot

Spring Boot provides several ways to configure CORS.

Global CORS Configuration

Apply CORS settings globally to all endpoints.

```
import org.springframework.context.annotation.Bean;
import
org.springframework.context.annotation.Configuration
;
import
org.springframework.web.servlet.config.annotation.Co
rsRegistry;
import
org.springframework.web.servlet.config.annotation.We
bMvcConfigurer;


@Configuration
```

```
public class WebConfig {

    @Bean
    public WebMvcConfigurer corsConfigurer() {
        return new WebMvcConfigurer() {
            @Override
            public void addCorsMappings(CorsRegistry
registry) {
                registry.addMapping("/**")

.allowedOrigins("http://localhost:3000")
                    .allowedMethods("GET",
"POST", "PUT", "DELETE")
                    .allowedHeaders("*")
                    .allowCredentials(true);
            }
        };
    }
}
```

Controller-Level CORS Configuration

Apply CORS settings to specific controllers or endpoints.

```
import
org.springframework.web.bind.annotation.CrossOrigin;
```

```java
import
org.springframework.web.bind.annotation.GetMapping;
import
org.springframework.web.bind.annotation.RestControll
er;

@RestController
@CrossOrigin(origins = "http://localhost:3000")
public class ProductController {

    @GetMapping("/products")
    public List<String> getProducts() {
        return List.of("Product 1", "Product 2",
"Product 3");
    }
}
```

Fetching Data with Axios or Fetch API

The frontend often needs to fetch data from the
backend for rendering dynamic content. You can use
either **Axios** or the native **Fetch API** for this purpose.

1. Installing Axios

Install Axios in your React project:

```
npm install axios
```

2. Fetching Data Using Axios

Example of fetching product data from a Spring Boot backend:

```javascript
import React, { useState, useEffect } from 'react';
import axios from 'axios';

function ProductList() {
    const [products, setProducts] = useState([]);
    const [error, setError] = useState(null);

    useEffect(() => {
        axios.get('http://localhost:8080/products')
            .then((response) => {
                setProducts(response.data);
            })
            .catch((error) => {
                setError(error.message);
            });
    }, []);
```

```jsx
    if (error) {
        return <p>Error: {error}</p>;
    }

    return (
        <ul>
            {products.map((product, index) => (
                <li key={index}>{product}</li>
            ))}
        </ul>
    );
}
export default ProductList;
```

3. Fetching Data Using Fetch API

The Fetch API is a built-in JavaScript feature for making HTTP requests.

```jsx
import React, { useState, useEffect } from 'react';

function ProductList() {
    const [products, setProducts] = useState([]);
    const [error, setError] = useState(null);
```

```jsx
    useEffect(() => {
        fetch('http://localhost:8080/products')
            .then((response) => {
                if (!response.ok) {
                    throw     new     Error('Network
response was not ok');
                }
                return response.json();
            })
            .then((data) => {
                setProducts(data);
            })
            .catch((error) => {
                setError(error.message);
            });
    }, []);

    if (error) {
        return <p>Error: {error}</p>;
    }

    return (
        <ul>
            {products.map((product, index) => (
                <li key={index}>{product}</li>
```

```
              ) ) }
        </ul>

    );

}


export default ProductList;
```

Sending Form Data and Handling Responses

The frontend frequently needs to send form data to the backend. This data is often used to create or update resources on the server.

1. Creating a Form in React

Build a simple form to submit product data:

```
import React, { useState } from 'react';
import axios from 'axios';

function ProductForm() {
    const [name, setName] = useState('');
    const [price, setPrice] = useState('');
    const [message, setMessage] = useState('');

    const handleSubmit = (event) => {
```

```
        event.preventDefault();

        const product = { name, price };

        axios.post('http://localhost:8080/products',
product)
            .then((response) => {
                setMessage('Product          created
successfully!');
            })
            .catch((error) => {
                setMessage('Failed       to       create
product: ' + error.message);
            });
    };

    return (
        <div>
            <form onSubmit={handleSubmit}>
                <div>
                    <label>Product Name:</label>
                    <input
                        type="text"
                        value={name}
```

```jsx
                    onChange={(e)                      =>
setName(e.target.value)}
                    required
                />
            </div>
            <div>
                <label>Product Price:</label>
                <input
                    type="number"
                    value={price}
                    onChange={(e)                      =>
setPrice(e.target.value)}
                    required
                />
            </div>
            <button          type="submit">Create
Product</button>
        </form>
        {message && <p>{message}</p>}
    </div>
  );
}

export default ProductForm;
```

2. Handling Form Data in Spring Boot

Spring Boot processes incoming JSON data using `@RequestBody`.

Controller Method for Handling Product Creation:

```java
import org.springframework.web.bind.annotation.*;
import java.util.HashMap;
import java.util.Map;

@RestController
@RequestMapping("/products")
public class ProductController {

    @PostMapping
    public                Map<String,                String>
createProduct(@RequestBody Product product) {
        // Simulate saving the product
        System.out.println("Product   Created:   "   +
product);
        Map<String,    String>    response    =    new
HashMap<>();
        response.put("message",    "Product    created
successfully!");
        return response;
    }
```

```
}
```

Product Entity:

```java
public class Product {
    private String name;
    private double price;

    // Getters and Setters
}
```

Best Practices for Connecting React and Spring Boot

Use **environment variables** to manage backend URLs, especially in production:

Create a `.env` file:

```
REACT_APP_API_URL=http://localhost:8080
```

Access in React:

```
const apiUrl = process.env.REACT_APP_API_URL;
```

- Always handle errors on both the backend and frontend for better user experience.

- Use appropriate HTTP methods (GET, POST, PUT, DELETE) to align with REST principles.

- Test CORS configuration thoroughly to ensure cross-origin requests work as expected.
- Keep your frontend and backend decoupled for better scalability and maintainability.

In this chapter, you've learned to configure CORS in Spring Boot, fetch data using Axios or Fetch API, and handle form submissions between React and Spring Boot. These skills will enable you to build dynamic, responsive, and data-driven applications.

Key Takeaways

CORS Understanding: Comprehensive understanding of Cross-Origin Resource Sharing (CORS) and how to configure it in Spring Boot to enable secure communication between frontend and backend.

Data Fetching Methods: Proficiency in using Axios and Fetch API for retrieving and sending data between React and Spring Boot applications.

Integration Best Practices: Best practices for connecting React with Spring Boot, including handling form data, managing responses, and ensuring seamless data flow.

Journal Exercises

1. **CORS Configuration:** Explain the concept of CORS and why it's important when connecting React with Spring Boot. How did you configure it in your application?

_____

_____

_____

_____

_____

_____

_____

2. **Data Fetching Techniques:** Compare using Axios versus the Fetch API for data retrieval. Which one did you prefer and why?

_____

_____

_____

_____

_____

_____

3. **Form Data Handling:** Implement a form in React that sends data to the Spring Boot backend. Document the process and any issues encountered during response handling.

_____

_____

_____

_____

CHAPTER 10

REAL-TIME UPDATES WITH WEBSOCKETS

Modern web applications often require real-time communication to provide dynamic and engaging user experiences. **WebSockets** are a powerful technology for enabling bi-directional communication between clients and servers. This chapter introduces WebSockets, explains how to add WebSocket support in Spring Boot, and guides you through building a real-time chat application using React.

Introduction to WebSockets

1. What Are WebSockets?

WebSockets provide a persistent, bi-directional communication channel between a client and a server over a single TCP connection. Unlike traditional HTTP requests, WebSockets maintain an open connection, allowing real-time data exchange.

2. Key Features of WebSockets

- **Low Latency**: Instantaneous communication compared to traditional polling or long-polling methods.

- **Bi-Directional**: Both client and server can send and receive messages simultaneously.

- **Event-Driven**: Ideal for applications requiring real-time updates, like chat systems, live notifications, and stock price tracking.

3. WebSocket Workflow

- The client initiates a WebSocket handshake using an HTTP request.

- The server upgrades the connection to the WebSocket protocol.

- The connection remains open, allowing continuous data exchange.

Adding WebSocket Support in Spring Boot

Spring Boot makes it easy to implement WebSocket communication using the **Spring WebSocket module**.

1. Add Dependencies

Include the following dependencies in your `pom.xml`:

```xml
<dependency>
    <groupId>org.springframework.boot</groupId>
    <artifactId>spring-boot-starter-
websocket</artifactId>
</dependency>
```

2. Create a WebSocket Configuration

Define a configuration class to enable WebSocket support and register endpoints.

```java
import
org.springframework.context.annotation.Configuration
;
import
org.springframework.web.socket.config.annotation.Ena
bleWebSocketMessageBroker;
import
org.springframework.web.socket.config.annotation.Sto
mpEndpointRegistry;
```

```java
import
org.springframework.web.socket.config.annotation.Web
SocketMessageBrokerConfigurer;

@Configuration
@EnableWebSocketMessageBroker
public      class      WebSocketConfig      implements
WebSocketMessageBrokerConfigurer {

    @Override
    public                                            void
registerStompEndpoints(StompEndpointRegistry
registry) {

registry.addEndpoint("/ws").setAllowedOrigins("http:
//localhost:3000").withSockJS();
    }

    @Override
    public                                            void
configureMessageBroker(org.springframework.messaging
.simp.config.MessageBrokerRegistry registry) {
        registry.enableSimpleBroker("/topic");

registry.setApplicationDestinationPrefixes("/app");
```

```
        }
}
```

- **/ws**: The WebSocket endpoint where the client connects.
- **/topic**: The prefix for topics (broadcast messages).
- **/app**: The prefix for messages sent to the server.

3. Create a Controller for Handling Messages

The controller processes incoming messages and broadcasts updates to subscribers.

```
import
org.springframework.messaging.handler.annotation.Mes
sageMapping;
import
org.springframework.messaging.handler.annotation.Sen
dTo;
import org.springframework.stereotype.Controller;

@Controller
public class ChatController {
```

```
@MessageMapping("/chat")
@SendTo("/topic/messages")
public String handleMessage(String message) {
    return message; // Broadcast the message to
all subscribers
    }
}
```

Building a Real-Time Chat Application with React

1. Install Required Libraries

Install `sockjs-client` and `@stomp/stompjs` for WebSocket communication:

```
npm install sockjs-client @stomp/stompjs
```

2. Create the Chat Component

Chat.js

```
import React, { useState, useEffect } from 'react';
import { over } from '@stomp/stompjs';
import SockJS from 'sockjs-client';

const Chat = () => {
```

```
    const    [stompClient,    setStompClient]    =
useState(null);
    const [messages, setMessages] = useState([]);
    const [input, setInput] = useState('');

    useEffect(() => {
        // Connect to the WebSocket server
        const           sock          =          new
SockJS('http://localhost:8080/ws');
        const client = over(sock);

        client.connect({}, () => {
            console.log('Connected to WebSocket');

            client.subscribe('/topic/messages',
(message) => {
                setMessages((prev)    =>    [...prev,
JSON.parse(message.body)]);
            });
        });

        setStompClient(client);

        return () => {
            if (client) client.disconnect();
```

```jsx
            };
        }, []);

        const sendMessage = () => {
            if (stompClient && input.trim()) {
                stompClient.send('/app/chat',            {},
JSON.stringify(input));
                setInput('');
            }
        };

        return (
            <div>
                <h1>Real-Time Chat</h1>
                <div style={{ border: '1px solid black',
padding: '10px', height: '300px', overflowY: 'scroll'
}}>
                    {messages.map((msg, index) => (
                        <div key={index}>{msg}</div>
                    ))}
                </div>
                <input
                    type="text"
                    value={input}
```

```
                onChange={ (e)                              =>
setInput(e.target.value) }
                placeholder="Type a message"
        />
        <button
onClick={sendMessage}>Send</button>
    </div>
    );
};


export default Chat;
```

3. Key Points in the Code

Connection: The `SockJS` client establishes a WebSocket connection to the Spring Boot endpoint (`/ws`).

Subscriptions: The client subscribes to the `/topic/messages` topic to receive real-time updates.

Sending Messages: Messages are sent to the `/app/chat` destination, which maps to the controller.

Testing the Real-Time Chat Application

Start the Spring Boot backend:

```
mvn spring-boot:run
```

Start the React frontend:

```
npm start
```

Open the chat application in multiple browser windows or tabs and send messages. Messages should appear in real-time across all connected clients.

Enhancements for Production

1. **Authentication**: Secure the WebSocket connection with authentication tokens.
2. **Persistent Storage**: Save chat messages to a database for historical records.
3. **Scalability**: Use a message broker like RabbitMQ or Kafka for distributed systems.
4. **UI Improvements**: Add timestamps, user names, and typing indicators for a polished chat experience.

Summary

In this chapter, you learned about WebSockets, how to configure them in Spring Boot, and how to build a real-time chat application with React. By combining WebSocket capabilities with Spring Boot and React, you can implement interactive and real-time features in your applications, enhancing user engagement and satisfaction.

Key Takeaways

WebSockets Introduction: Understanding the fundamentals of WebSockets and their role in enabling real-time, bidirectional communication between clients and servers.

Real-Time Application Development: Skills in building real-time applications, such as chat apps, using React for the frontend and Spring Boot for the backend with WebSocket integration.

Enhancements for Production: Knowledge of best practices and enhancements required to transition real-time applications from development to production environments.

Journal Exercises

1. **WebSockets Basics:** Describe how WebSockets differ from traditional HTTP requests. What are the advantages of using WebSockets for real-time applications?

_____

_____

_____

_____

_____

_____

_____

2. **Building a Chat Application:** Develop a simple real-time chat application using React and Spring Boot

with WebSockets. What challenges did you face during development and testing?

_____

_____

_____

_____

_____

_____

_____

3. **Production Enhancements:** Propose enhancements to your chat application to make it production-ready. Consider aspects like scalability, security, and user experience.

_____

_____

_____

_____

NOTE

PART 4

ADVANCED FULL STACK DEVELOPMENT

CHAPTER 11

MICROSERVICES ARCHITECTURE

Microservices architecture is a design paradigm for building complex and scalable applications by dividing them into smaller, loosely coupled, and independently deployable services. This chapter explores microservices in Spring Boot, demonstrates how to implement a simple microservices application, and delves into essential tools like **Spring Cloud Netflix Eureka** for service discovery and an **API Gateway** for routing and load balancing.

Understanding Microservices in Spring Boot

1. What Are Microservices?

Microservices are a collection of small, independent services that work together to form a larger application. Each service is designed to perform a specific business function and communicates with other services through lightweight protocols like HTTP or messaging queues.

2. Key Characteristics of Microservices

- **Independent Deployability**: Each service can be deployed independently without affecting others.
- **Loose Coupling**: Services interact minimally with each other, often through APIs.
- **Scalability**: Individual services can be scaled independently based on their load.
- **Technology Diversity**: Different services can use different programming languages, databases, or frameworks.

3. Benefits of Microservices

Improved fault isolation: Failures in one service do not bring down the entire system.

Enhanced agility and flexibility in development and deployment.

Easier scaling and maintenance for large applications.

4. Challenges of Microservices

- Increased complexity in deployment and monitoring.

- Managing inter-service communication and data consistency.
- Ensuring proper security and error handling across services.

Implementing a Simple Microservices Application

Let's create a microservices system with two services:

1. **Product Service**: Manages product data.
2. **Order Service**: Manages orders and fetches product data from the Product Service.

1. Setting Up the Product Service

Dependencies

Add the following dependencies to `pom.xml`:

```xml
<dependency>
    <groupId>org.springframework.boot</groupId>
    <artifactId>spring-boot-starter-web</artifactId>
</dependency>
<dependency>
    <groupId>org.springframework.cloud</groupId>
    <artifactId>spring-cloud-starter-netflix-eureka-client</artifactId>
```

```
</dependency>
```

Controller for Product Service

```java
import
org.springframework.web.bind.annotation.GetMapping;
import
org.springframework.web.bind.annotation.RequestParam
;
import
org.springframework.web.bind.annotation.RestControll
er;

import java.util.Map;

@RestController
public class ProductController {

    private final Map<String, String> productData =
Map.of(
            "1", "Laptop",
            "2", "Smartphone",
            "3", "Tablet"
    );
```

```
    @GetMapping("/product")
    public String getProduct(@RequestParam String id)
{
        return productData.getOrDefault(id, "Product
not found");
    }
}
```

2. Setting Up the Order Service

Dependencies

Add the same dependencies as the Product Service.

Controller for Order Service

The Order Service fetches product data from the
Product Service.

```
import
org.springframework.web.bind.annotation.GetMapping;
import
org.springframework.web.bind.annotation.RequestParam
;
import
org.springframework.web.bind.annotation.RestControll
er;
import org.springframework.web.client.RestTemplate;
```

```
@RestController
public class OrderController {

    private final RestTemplate restTemplate;

    public                OrderController(RestTemplate
restTemplate) {
        this.restTemplate = restTemplate;
    }

    @GetMapping("/order")
    public String createOrder(@RequestParam String
productId) {
        String           product           =
restTemplate.getForObject("http://PRODUCT-
SERVICE/product?id=" + productId, String.class);
        return "Order created for: " + product;
    }
}
```

Bean Configuration for RestTemplate

```
import org.springframework.context.annotation.Bean;
```

```java
import
org.springframework.context.annotation.Configuration
;
import org.springframework.web.client.RestTemplate;

@Configuration
public class AppConfig {

    @Bean
    public RestTemplate restTemplate() {
        return new RestTemplate();
    }
}
```

Service Discovery with Spring Cloud Netflix Eureka

Service discovery allows services to register themselves and discover other services dynamically, eliminating the need for hardcoded service URLs.

1. **Setting Up Eureka Server**

Dependencies

Add the Eureka Server dependency to `pom.xml`:

```xml
<dependency>
    <groupId>org.springframework.cloud</groupId>
```

```
    <artifactId>spring-cloud-starter-netflix-eureka-
server</artifactId>
</dependency>
```

Eureka Server Configuration

Create a Spring Boot application for the Eureka Server.
Annotate the main class:

```
import org.springframework.boot.SpringApplication;
import
org.springframework.boot.autoconfigure.SpringBootApp
lication;
import
org.springframework.cloud.netflix.eureka.server.Enab
leEurekaServer;

@SpringBootApplication
@EnableEurekaServer
public class EurekaServerApplication {
    public static void main(String[] args) {

SpringApplication.run(EurekaServerApplication.class,
args);
    }
}
```

Application Properties for Eureka Server

```
server.port=8761
eureka.client.register-with-eureka=false
eureka.client.fetch-registry=false
```

Start the Eureka Server and visit `http://localhost:8761` to see the dashboard.

2. Register Product and Order Services

Add Eureka Client Dependency

Add this dependency to both services:

```
<dependency>
    <groupId>org.springframework.cloud</groupId>
    <artifactId>spring-cloud-starter-netflix-eureka-client</artifactId>
</dependency>
```

Application Properties

For Product Service:

```
server.port=8081
eureka.client.service-url.default-zone=http://localhost:8761/eureka
spring.application.name=PRODUCT-SERVICE
```

For Order Service:

```
server.port=8082
eureka.client.service-url.default-
zone=http://localhost:8761/eureka
spring.application.name=ORDER-SERVICE
```

The services will register themselves with the Eureka Server.

API Gateway and Load Balancing

1. Setting Up API Gateway

An API Gateway routes requests to appropriate microservices and handles cross-cutting concerns like authentication and rate limiting.

Dependencies

Add Spring Cloud Gateway dependency:

```
<dependency>
    <groupId>org.springframework.cloud</groupId>
    <artifactId>spring-cloud-starter-
gateway</artifactId>
</dependency>
<dependency>
    <groupId>org.springframework.cloud</groupId>
```

```
    <artifactId>spring-cloud-starter-netflix-eureka-
client</artifactId>
</dependency>
```

API Gateway Configuration

```
import org.springframework.boot.SpringApplication;
import
org.springframework.boot.autoconfigure.SpringBootApp
lication;

@SpringBootApplication
public class ApiGatewayApplication {
    public static void main(String[] args) {

SpringApplication.run(ApiGatewayApplication.class,
args);
    }
}
```

application.properties

```
spring.application.name=API-GATEWAY
server.port=8080
eureka.client.service-url.default-
zone=http://localhost:8761/eureka
```

```
spring.cloud.gateway.routes[0].id=product-service
spring.cloud.gateway.routes[0].uri=lb://PRODUCT-
SERVICE
spring.cloud.gateway.routes[0].predicates[0]=Path=/p
roduct/**

spring.cloud.gateway.routes[1].id=order-service
spring.cloud.gateway.routes[1].uri=lb://ORDER-
SERVICE
spring.cloud.gateway.routes[1].predicates[0]=Path=/o
rder/**
```

2. Load Balancing with Eureka

The API Gateway uses Eureka for service discovery and load balances requests across multiple instances of a service.

Testing the Microservices Architecture

Start the Eureka Server (`mvn spring-boot:run`).
Start the Product Service and Order Service.
Start the API Gateway.

Access endpoints via the API Gateway:

- `http://localhost:8080/product?id=1`
- `http://localhost:8080/order?productId=1`

Summary

In this chapter, you've learned the fundamentals of microservices architecture, implemented a basic microservices application, set up service discovery with Eureka, and built an API Gateway for routing and load balancing. These concepts form the backbone of scalable and maintainable distributed systems.

Key Takeaways

Microservices Understanding: Deep understanding of microservices architecture, its benefits, and how it contrasts with monolithic systems.

Service Implementation: Practical experience in building individual microservices (e.g., Product and Order services) using Spring Boot.

Service Discovery and API Gateway: Proficiency in setting up service discovery using Spring Cloud Netflix Eureka and implementing an API Gateway for efficient load balancing and request management.

Journal Exercises

1. **Microservices Fundamentals:** Explain the key characteristics of a microservices architecture. How does it differ from a monolithic architecture?

_____

_____

_____

_____

_____

_____

_____

_____

2. **Building Services:** Create simple Product and Order services using Spring Boot. Document the steps and any integration issues you encountered.

_____

_____

_____

_____

_____

_____

_____

3. **Service Discovery with Eureka:** Set up a Eureka Server and register your Product and Order services. How does service discovery facilitate communication in a microservices ecosystem?

_____

_____

_____

_____

_____

_____

_____

4. **API Gateway Implementation:** Implement an API Gateway for your microservices. What benefits does an API Gateway provide in terms of load balancing and request routing?

_____

_____

_____

_____

_____

_____

_____

CHAPTER 12

PERFORMANCE OPTIMIZATION

Optimizing performance is critical to ensuring a smooth user experience and efficient system operations. This chapter covers best practices for optimizing Spring Boot APIs, reducing React bundle sizes, and implementing caching with Redis and Spring Cache.

Optimizing Spring Boot APIs

1. Enable HTTP Compression

HTTP compression reduces the size of data sent between the server and client, improving API response times.

Configuration:

Add the following to `application.properties` to enable GZIP compression:

```
server.compression.enabled=true
server.compression.mime-
types=application/json,application/xml,text/html,tex
t/xml,text/plain
server.compression.min-response-size=1024
```

- **server.compression.enabled**: Enables compression.
- **server.compression.mime-types**: Specifies the types of content to compress.
- **server.compression.min-response-size**: Sets the minimum response size for compression.

2. Use Pageable for Large Data Sets

Returning large data sets in a single request can degrade performance. Use pagination to fetch data in chunks.

Controller Example:

```
import org.springframework.data.domain.Page;
import org.springframework.data.domain.Pageable;
import
org.springframework.web.bind.annotation.GetMapping;
import
org.springframework.web.bind.annotation.RestControll
er;

@RestController
public class ProductController {
```

```java
    private          final          ProductRepository
productRepository;

    public          ProductController(ProductRepository
productRepository) {
        this.productRepository = productRepository;
    }


    @GetMapping("/products")
    public     Page<Product>     getProducts(Pageable
pageable) {
        return productRepository.findAll(pageable);
    }
}
```

Repository Example:

```java
import
org.springframework.data.jpa.repository.JpaRepositor
y;


public    interface    ProductRepository    extends
JpaRepository<Product, Long> {
}
```

Client Request Example:

```
GET /products?page=0&size=10
```

3. Optimize Database Queries

Use Projections: Fetch only the required fields.

```java
public interface ProductProjection {
    String getName();
    double getPrice();
}


@Query("SELECT p.name AS name, p.price AS price FROM
Product p")
List<ProductProjection> findAllProjectedBy();
```

Enable Query Caching:

Use Hibernate's second-level cache to store query results.

Add the dependency:

```xml
<dependency>
    <groupId>org.springframework.boot</groupId>
    <artifactId>spring-boot-starter-data-jpa</artifactId>
</dependency>
```

Configure in `application.properties`:

```
spring.jpa.properties.hibernate.cache.use_second_lev
el_cache=true
spring.jpa.properties.hibernate.cache.region.factory
_class=org.hibernate.cache.jcache.JCacheRegionFactor
y
```

4. Profile Your Application

Use tools like **Spring Boot Actuator** and **JProfiler** to analyze bottlenecks and optimize resource usage.

Add Actuator Dependency:

```xml
<dependency>
    <groupId>org.springframework.boot</groupId>
    <artifactId>spring-boot-starter-
actuator</artifactId>
</dependency>
```

Reducing React Bundle Sizes

1. Tree Shaking

Tree shaking eliminates unused code during the build process.

Ensure your project uses ES6 modules (`import/export`).

Use Webpack or Vite, which have tree-shaking capabilities by default.

2. Code Splitting

Code splitting breaks the JavaScript bundle into smaller chunks, loading only the necessary code for a given route.

React Example:

```javascript
import React, { Suspense, lazy } from 'react';
const Home = lazy(() => import('./Home'));
const About = lazy(() => import('./About'));

function App() {
    return (
        <Suspense fallback={<div>Loading...</div>}>
            <Switch>
                <Route path="/home" component={Home} />
                <Route path="/about" component={About} />
            </Switch>
        </Suspense>
```

```
    );
}
```

3. Use Production Builds

Ensure React is running in production mode to optimize performance.

Build your project with:

```
npm run build
```

Serve the optimized bundle from the `build` directory.

4. Minify CSS and JS

Tools like Webpack automatically minify CSS and JavaScript during the build process. Use tools like `Terser` for further optimization.

5. Lazy Loading Images

Use libraries like `react-lazyload` to delay loading images until they are in the viewport.

```
import React from 'react';
import LazyLoad from 'react-lazyload';
```

```
function ImageGallery() {
    return (
        <div>
            <LazyLoad height={200} offset={100}>
                <img              src="large-image.jpg"
alt="Large Image" />
            </LazyLoad>
        </div>
    );
}
```

Caching with Redis and Spring Cache

Caching is a technique to store frequently accessed data in memory, reducing database load and improving response times.

1. Setting Up Redis

Install Redis:

On Linux:

```
sudo apt install redis
```

On Windows: Use Docker or download Redis binaries.

Add Redis Dependency:

```xml
<dependency>
    <groupId>org.springframework.boot</groupId>
    <artifactId>spring-boot-starter-data-redis</artifactId>
</dependency>
```

2. Enable Spring Cache

Spring Boot provides caching support out of the box.

Add Cache Configuration:

```java
import org.springframework.cache.annotation.EnableCaching;
import org.springframework.context.annotation.Configuration;

@Configuration
@EnableCaching
public class CacheConfig {
}
```

Update `application.properties`:

```
spring.cache.type=redis
spring.redis.host=localhost
spring.redis.port=6379
```

3. Using @Cacheable Annotation

The `@Cacheable` annotation stores the result of a method in the cache.

Service Example:

```
import
org.springframework.cache.annotation.Cacheable;
import org.springframework.stereotype.Service;

@Service
public class ProductService {

    @Cacheable("products")
    public String getProductById(String id) {
        simulateSlowService();
        return "Product " + id;
    }

    private void simulateSlowService() {
        try {
```

```java
            Thread.sleep(3000); // Simulates a delay
        } catch (InterruptedException e) {
            Thread.currentThread().interrupt();
        }
    }
}
```

Controller Example:

```java
import
org.springframework.web.bind.annotation.GetMapping;
import
org.springframework.web.bind.annotation.RequestParam
;
import
org.springframework.web.bind.annotation.RestControll
er;

@RestController
public class ProductController {

    private final ProductService productService;

    public            ProductController(ProductService
productService) {
```

```
        this.productService = productService;
    }


    @GetMapping("/product")
    public String getProduct(@RequestParam String id)
{

        return productService.getProductById(id);

    }

}
```

4. Evicting Cached Data

Use the `@CacheEvict` annotation to remove stale cache entries.

```
@CacheEvict(value = "products", allEntries = true)
public void clearCache() {
    // Cache cleared
}
```

Summary

In this chapter, you've learned how to:

- Optimize Spring Boot APIs using techniques like HTTP compression and pagination.

- Reduce React bundle sizes through tree shaking, code splitting, and lazy loading.
- Implement caching with Redis and Spring Cache to improve response times and reduce server load.

By applying these strategies, you can build high-performance applications that deliver a seamless experience to users.

Key Takeaways

Spring Boot API Optimization: Techniques for enhancing the performance of Spring Boot APIs, including efficient coding practices and leveraging Spring Boot features.

Reducing React Bundle Sizes: Strategies for minimizing the size of React application bundles to improve load times and overall performance.

Caching with Redis and Spring Cache: Understanding the implementation and benefits of caching mechanisms using Redis and Spring Cache to accelerate data retrieval and reduce server load.

Journal Exercises

1. **API Optimization Techniques:** Identify and implement three strategies to optimize Spring Boot APIs. Measure their impact on performance.

_____

_____

_____

_____

_____

_____

_____

_____

2. **React Bundle Size Reduction:** Analyze your React application's bundle size. What steps can you take to reduce it without compromising functionality?

_____

_____

_____

_____

_____

_____

_____

3. **Caching Strategies:** Integrate Redis with Spring Cache in your application. How does caching improve performance, and what considerations must be made for cache invalidation?

_____

_____

_____

_____

_____

_____

CHAPTER 13

TESTING AND DEBUGGING

Testing and debugging are critical for ensuring the quality and reliability of full stack applications. This chapter explores how to write **unit and integration tests in Spring Boot**, test React components using **Jest** and **React Testing Library**, and apply effective debugging techniques for full stack applications.

Unit and Integration Testing in Spring Boot

1. Importance of Testing in Spring Boot

Unit Tests: Validate individual components (e.g., services, controllers) in isolation.

Integration Tests: Ensure multiple components work together correctly, including database interactions and API responses.

2. Setting Up Testing Dependencies

Spring Boot includes testing tools out of the box. Add the following dependencies to `pom.xml`:

```xml
<dependency>
    <groupId>org.springframework.boot</groupId>
    <artifactId>spring-boot-starter-test</artifactId>
    <scope>test</scope>
</dependency>
```

This includes libraries like JUnit 5, AssertJ, and Mockito.

3. Writing Unit Tests

Service Layer Test Example

```java
import static org.assertj.core.api.Assertions.assertThat;

import org.junit.jupiter.api.Test;
import org.mockito.InjectMocks;
import org.mockito.Mock;
import org.mockito.MockitoAnnotations;

public class ProductServiceTest {

    @Mock
```

```java
    private ProductRepository productRepository;

    @InjectMocks
    private ProductService productService;

    public ProductServiceTest() {
        MockitoAnnotations.openMocks(this);
    }

    @Test
    public void testGetProductById() {
        Product product = new Product(1L, "Laptop",
1200.00);

when(productRepository.findById(1L)).thenReturn(Opti
onal.of(product));

        Product                result          =
productService.getProductById(1L);


assertThat(result.getName()).isEqualTo("Laptop");

assertThat(result.getPrice()).isEqualTo(1200.00);
    }
```

```
}
```

Explanation:

- **Mockito:** Mock dependencies like `ProductRepository` to isolate the `ProductService` logic.
- **Assertions:** Validate the expected output using AssertJ.

4. Writing Integration Tests

Integration Test for REST Controller

Use `@SpringBootTest` and `MockMvc` for testing APIs.

```
import                                      static
org.springframework.test.web.servlet.request.MockMvc
RequestBuilders.get;
import                                      static
org.springframework.test.web.servlet.result.MockMvcR
esultMatchers.status;
import                                      static
org.springframework.test.web.servlet.result.MockMvcR
esultMatchers.jsonPath;
```

```java
import org.junit.jupiter.api.Test;
import
org.springframework.beans.factory.annotation.Autowir
ed;
import
org.springframework.boot.test.autoconfigure.web.serv
let.AutoConfigureMockMvc;
import
org.springframework.boot.test.context.SpringBootTest
;

@SpringBootTest
@AutoConfigureMockMvc
public class ProductControllerIntegrationTest {

    @Autowired
    private MockMvc mockMvc;

    @Test
    public void testGetProductById() throws Exception
{
        mockMvc.perform(get("/product?id=1"))
                .andExpect(status().isOk())
```

```
    .andExpect(jsonPath("$.name").value("Laptop"));
    }
}
```

Explanation:

- **@SpringBootTest**: Boots the entire application context for integration testing.

- **MockMvc**: Simulates HTTP requests and validates responses.

Testing React Components with Jest and React Testing Library

1. Setting Up Testing Tools

Install Jest and React Testing Library in your React project:

```
npm install --save-dev jest @testing-library/react
@testing-library/jest-dom
```

Add the following script to **package.json** to run tests:

```
"scripts": {
```

```
    "test": "react-scripts test"
}
```

2. Writing Tests for React Components

Unit Test for a Button Component

```
import React from 'react';
import { render, screen } from '@testing-
library/react';
import Button from './Button';

test('renders button with correct label', () => {
    render(<Button label="Click Me" />);
    const buttonElement = screen.getByText(/Click
Me/i);
    expect(buttonElement).toBeInTheDocument();
});
```

Explanation:

- **render**: Renders the component in a virtual DOM.

- **screen.getByText**: Finds an element based on text content.

- **expect**: Asserts that the button is present in the DOM.

Integration Test for a Form Component

```
import React from 'react';
import { render, fireEvent, screen } from '@testing-library/react';
import Form from './Form';

test('submits form with correct data', () => {
    const handleSubmit = jest.fn();

    render(<Form onSubmit={handleSubmit} />);
    fireEvent.change(screen.getByLabelText(/name/i),
{ target: { value: 'John' } });

fireEvent.change(screen.getByLabelText(/email/i),   {
target: { value: 'john@example.com' } });
    fireEvent.click(screen.getByText(/submit/i));

    expect(handleSubmit).toHaveBeenCalledWith({
name: 'John', email: 'john@example.com' });
});
```

Explanation:

- `fireEvent`: Simulates user interactions like typing and clicking.
- `jest.fn`: Mocks a callback function to validate form submissions.

Debugging Techniques for Full Stack Applications

1. Debugging in Spring Boot

Using IntelliJ IDEA or Eclipse Debugger

- Set breakpoints in your code and run the application in debug mode (`mvn spring-boot:run -Ddebug`).
- Inspect variables, step through code, and analyze method calls.

Enable Detailed Logs

Adjust logging levels in `application.properties`:

```
logging.level.org.springframework=DEBUG
logging.level.com.example=TRACE
```

Analyze HTTP Requests

Use tools like **Postman** or **curl** to simulate API requests and validate responses.

2. Debugging in React

Using Browser Developer Tools

Open the developer tools in Chrome or Firefox.

Inspect React components using the **React Developer Tools** extension.

Monitor network requests under the **Network** tab.

Debugging with `console.log`

Insert `console.log` statements to log state and props at different points in your components.

3. Debugging Full Stack Integration

Cross-Origin Issues

Ensure **CORS** is correctly configured in Spring Boot.

Debug CORS errors using the browser's **Console** tab.

Analyze Network Traffic

Use tools like **Postman**, **Fiddler**, or **Wireshark** to debug API requests and responses.

Error Tracking Tools

Integrate error monitoring tools like **Sentry** or **New Relic** for real-time issue tracking.

Best Practices for Testing and Debugging

Write **unit tests** for critical functions and **integration tests** for end-to-end flows.

Automate tests with tools like Jenkins or GitHub Actions to ensure continuous quality.

Use meaningful logging levels (INFO, DEBUG, ERROR) to streamline debugging.

Regularly review and update tests to reflect changes in the application.

Summary

In this chapter, you've learned how to write unit and integration tests for Spring Boot, test React components using Jest and React Testing Library, and debug full stack applications effectively. These practices ensure your applications are robust, reliable, and maintainable.

Key Takeaways

Comprehensive Testing: Skills in writing and executing unit and integration tests for Spring Boot applications to ensure functionality and reliability.

React Component Testing: Proficiency in testing React components using tools like Jest and React Testing Library, enhancing code quality and maintainability.

Effective Debugging: Mastery of debugging techniques and best practices for identifying and resolving issues in full stack applications, ensuring smoother development cycles.

Journal Exercises

1. **Unit and Integration Testing:** Develop unit and integration tests for your Spring Boot services. Reflect on the importance of testing in ensuring application reliability.

_____

_____

_____

_____

_____

_____

_____

2. **React Component Testing:** Use Jest and React Testing Library to test your React components. What challenges did you face, and how did testing improve your code quality?

_____

_____

_____

_____

_____

_____

_____

_____

3. **Debugging Practices:** Document the debugging techniques you used while developing full stack applications. How did these techniques help in identifying and resolving issues?

_____

_____

_____

_____

_____

_____

PART 5

DEPLOYMENT AND SCALING

CHAPTER 14

DEPLOYING FULL STACK APPLICATIONS

Deploying a full stack application involves preparing the backend (Spring Boot) and frontend (React) for production and hosting them on reliable platforms. This chapter covers best practices for preparing Spring Boot for production, hosting React applications on platforms like **Netlify** or **Vercel**, and deploying the backend to cloud providers such as **AWS**, **Azure**, or **Heroku**.

Preparing Spring Boot for Production

1. Optimize Application Configuration

Set Up External Configuration

Use `application.properties` or `application.yml` for environment-specific settings.

Example:

```
server.port=8080
spring.datasource.url=jdbc:mysql://prod-database-
url:3306/mydb
```

```
spring.datasource.username=prod-user
spring.datasource.password=prod-password
```

Enable Profile-Specific Configurations

Spring Boot supports profiles (e.g., `dev, prod`) for environment-specific settings.

Example:

- Add profile-specific files: `application-prod.properties` and `application-dev.properties`.
- Activate the profile:

```
spring.profiles.active=prod
```

2. Secure Your Application

Use HTTPS

Configure HTTPS by adding an SSL certificate.

Steps:

Generate a keystore:

```
keytool -genkey -alias springboot -keyalg RSA -keystore keystore.jks
```

Configure in `application.properties`:

```
server.ssl.enabled=true
server.ssl.key-store=classpath:keystore.jks
server.ssl.key-store-password=yourpassword
```

Protect Sensitive Data

Store sensitive information (e.g., passwords, API keys) securely using environment variables or a secrets manager.

3. Optimize Performance

Enable Caching

Use Spring Cache with Redis or other caching solutions to reduce database load.

Example:

```
@Cacheable("products")
public List<Product> getAllProducts() {
    return productRepository.findAll();
}
```

Use a Connection Pool

Optimize database connections using connection pooling with HikariCP:

```
spring.datasource.hikari.maximum-pool-size=10
spring.datasource.hikari.minimum-idle=5
```

4. Package the Application

Build the Spring Boot application as a JAR or WAR:

```
mvn clean package
```

Hosting React Applications on Platforms like Netlify or Vercel

1. Build the React Application

Before deploying, build the production version of your React app:

```
npm run build
```

This generates an optimized `build` folder containing static assets.

2. Deploy to Netlify

Steps to Deploy

Log in to [Netlify](#).

Drag and drop the `build` folder into the deployment area, or link your GitHub repository.

Configure build settings if deploying from GitHub:

- Build command: `npm run build`
- Publish directory: `build`

Custom Domain and HTTPS

Set a custom domain and enable HTTPS with Netlify's free SSL.

3. Deploy to Vercel

Steps to Deploy

Log in to [Vercel](#).

Import your GitHub repository.

Configure build settings:

- Framework: `React`
- Build command: `npm run build`
- Output directory: `build`

Advantages of Vercel

- Built-in CI/CD for automatic deployments.
- Edge network for low-latency content delivery.

Deploying Backend to AWS, Azure, or Heroku

1. Deploying to AWS

Steps to Deploy with AWS Elastic Beanstalk

Install AWS CLI:

```
pip install awscli
```

Create an Elastic Beanstalk Environment:

- Log in to the AWS Management Console.
- Create an application and an environment.
- Select **Java** as the platform.

Deploy the JAR File:

- Upload the JAR file created during the Spring Boot build process.

Best Practices on AWS

- Use **Amazon RDS** for databases.

- Enable **Auto Scaling** for high availability.
- Use **CloudWatch** for monitoring logs and performance.

2. Deploying to Azure

Steps to Deploy on Azure App Service

Install Azure CLI:

```
az login
```

Create an App Service:

```
az webapp create --name my-springboot-app --resource-group myResourceGroup --plan myAppServicePlan
```

Deploy the JAR File:

```
az webapp deploy --resource-group myResourceGroup --name my-springboot-app --src-path target/myapp.jar
```

Best Practices on Azure

- Use **Azure Database for MySQL/PostgreSQL** for managed database services.

- Enable **Application Insights** for detailed monitoring.

3. Deploying to Heroku

Steps to Deploy on Heroku

Install Heroku CLI:

```
sudo snap install --classic heroku
```

Create a Heroku Application:

```
heroku create my-springboot-app
```

Deploy the JAR File:

Add a `Procfile` to the root directory:

```
web: java -jar target/myapp.jar
```

Deploy to Heroku:

```
git init
git add .
git commit -m "Initial commit"
git push heroku main
```

Advantages of Heroku

Simple deployment for small to medium-scale applications.

Free tier for testing and development.

Integrating Frontend and Backend

1. CORS Configuration for Production

Ensure the backend allows requests from the frontend domain:

```
spring.web.cors.allowed-
origins=https://myfrontenddomain.com
```

2. Environment Variables

Use environment variables to configure API URLs in React:

Add a **.env file**:

```
REACT_APP_API_URL=https://mybackenddomain.com
```

Best Practices for Deployment

- **Security**: Use HTTPS and protect sensitive data with environment variables.
- **Scaling**: Use cloud features like **Auto Scaling** and **Load Balancers**.
- **Monitoring**: Use tools like AWS CloudWatch, Azure Monitor, or Heroku Logs for real-time insights.
- **CI/CD**: Automate builds and deployments with pipelines (e.g., GitHub Actions, Jenkins).

Summary

This chapter covered the end-to-end deployment process for full stack applications. You learned how to prepare a Spring Boot backend for production, deploy a React frontend to platforms like Netlify or Vercel, and host the backend on cloud providers such as AWS, Azure, or Heroku. With these tools and practices, you can ensure your application is reliable, scalable, and ready for production.

Key Takeaways

Production-Ready Spring Boot: Knowledge of preparing and configuring Spring Boot applications for production environments, including security, performance, and scalability considerations.

Frontend Deployment: Understanding of deploying React applications to various hosting platforms, leveraging their features for optimal performance and reliability.

Backend Deployment to Cloud: Skills in deploying Spring Boot applications to cloud services like AWS, Azure, or Heroku, ensuring accessibility and scalability.

Integration Best Practices: Ensuring seamless integration between frontend and backend post-deployment, maintaining consistent communication and functionality.

Journal Exercises

1. **Production Preparation:** Outline the steps you took to prepare your Spring Boot application for production. What configurations and optimizations were necessary?

_____

_____

_____

_____

_____

_____

_____

_____

2. **Frontend Hosting:** Deploy your React application on platforms like Netlify or Vercel. Compare the deployment processes and performance metrics of each platform.

_____

_____

_____

_____

_____

_____

_____

_____

_____

3. **Backend Deployment:** Deploy your Spring Boot backend to cloud platforms such as AWS, Azure, or Heroku. Document any challenges and how you addressed them.

_____

_____

_____

_____

_____

_____

_____

_____

4. **Integration Review:** Ensure that the frontend and backend are correctly integrated post-deployment. What testing did you perform to confirm seamless interaction?

_____

_____

_____

_____

_____

_____

_____

CHAPTER 15

SCALING FULL STACK APPLICATIONS

Scaling a full stack application ensures it can handle increased user demand while maintaining performance, reliability, and availability. This chapter explores scaling the backend using **Docker** and **Kubernetes**, implementing load balancers and auto-scaling, and best practices for building a scalable full stack architecture.

Scaling Backend with Docker and Kubernetes

1. Containerization with Docker

Docker allows you to package your application and its dependencies into a portable container, enabling consistency across development, testing, and production environments.

1.1. Setting Up Docker for Spring Boot

Dockerfile for Spring Boot:

Create a **Dockerfile** in the root of your Spring Boot project.

```dockerfile
# Use a base image with Java
FROM openjdk:17-jdk-slim

# Set working directory
WORKDIR /app

# Copy the JAR file into the container
COPY target/myapp.jar app.jar

# Expose the application port
EXPOSE 8080

# Run the application
ENTRYPOINT ["java", "-jar", "app.jar"]
```

Build the Docker Image:

Run the following commands:

```
mvn clean package
docker build -t my-springboot-app .
```

Run the Container:

```
docker run -p 8080:8080 my-springboot-app
```

2. Orchestrating Containers with Kubernetes

Kubernetes automates the deployment, scaling, and management of containerized applications.

2.1. Setting Up Kubernetes

Install **kubectl** and a local Kubernetes cluster like **Minikube**.

Deploying the Spring Boot App:

Create a Deployment YAML:

Save this as `deployment.yaml`:

```yaml
apiVersion: apps/v1
kind: Deployment
metadata:
  name: springboot-app
spec:
  replicas: 3
  selector:
    matchLabels:
```

```
      app: springboot-app
  template:
    metadata:
      labels:
        app: springboot-app
    spec:
      containers:
      - name: springboot-app
        image: my-springboot-app
        ports:
        - containerPort: 8080
```

Create a Service YAML:

Save this as `service.yaml`:

```
apiVersion: v1
kind: Service
metadata:
  name: springboot-service
spec:
  type: NodePort
  selector:
    app: springboot-app
  ports:
  - protocol: TCP
```

```
    port: 80
    targetPort: 8080
    nodePort: 30080
```

Apply the Configurations:
```
kubectl apply -f deployment.yaml
kubectl apply -f service.yaml
```

Access **the** **Application**:

Access the app at `http://<node-ip>:30080`.

2.2. Benefits of Kubernetes

- Automatic scaling with Horizontal Pod Autoscaler.
- Self-healing with pod restarts on failure.
- Load balancing across replicas.

Implementing Load Balancers and Auto-Scaling

1. Load Balancers

Load balancers distribute incoming traffic across multiple servers or replicas to prevent overloading any single instance.

Types of Load Balancers

1. **Hardware Load Balancers**: High-performance physical devices.

2. **Software Load Balancers**: Solutions like NGINX or HAProxy.

3. **Cloud Load Balancers**: Services provided by AWS, Azure, or Google Cloud.

Using AWS Elastic Load Balancer (ELB)

1. Set up an **Application Load Balancer (ALB)** for HTTP and HTTPS traffic.

2. Configure target groups to register instances of your backend service.

3. Integrate with **Auto Scaling Groups** to dynamically add or remove instances based on traffic.

2. Auto-Scaling

Auto-scaling dynamically adjusts the number of application instances based on demand, ensuring efficient resource utilization.

2.1. Auto-Scaling in Kubernetes

Kubernetes provides the **Horizontal Pod Autoscaler (HPA)** to scale pods based on CPU or memory usage.

Enable HPA:

```
kubectl autoscale deployment springboot-app --cpu-percent=50 --min=1 --max=10
```

2.2. Auto-Scaling in AWS

1. Use **Auto Scaling Groups** to scale EC2 instances based on CloudWatch metrics (e.g., CPU utilization).
2. Define scaling policies for adding or removing instances automatically.

Best Practices for Scalable Full Stack Architecture

1. Design for Statelessness

- Use stateless services to make scaling easier.
- Store session data in external systems like Redis or databases.

2. Leverage Asynchronous Processing

- Offload heavy tasks to background workers using message queues like RabbitMQ or Kafka.
- Example: Process image uploads asynchronously to reduce response times.

3. Use Caching for Frequently Accessed Data

- Implement caching at multiple levels:
- **Database Caching**: Use Redis or Memcached for query results.
- **HTTP Response Caching**: Cache API responses with tools like Varnish or NGINX.
- **Browser Caching**: Configure `Cache-Control` headers.

4. Monitor and Optimize Performance

- Use tools like Prometheus and Grafana for real-time metrics and monitoring.
- Analyze logs with tools like ELK (Elasticsearch, Logstash, Kibana) stack or AWS CloudWatch.

5. Adopt CI/CD Pipelines

- Automate deployments and scaling adjustments with tools like Jenkins, GitHub Actions, or AWS CodePipeline.

6. Use Microservices Architecture

- Divide applications into smaller, independently scalable services.
- Use an API Gateway (e.g., AWS API Gateway, Kong) for routing and load balancing.

Summary

In this chapter, you've learned how to scale backend services using Docker and Kubernetes, implement load balancers and auto-scaling, and apply best practices for scalable full stack architecture. By adopting these strategies, your application can efficiently handle growing traffic and provide a seamless experience for users at any scale.

Key Takeaways

Containerization with Docker: Ability to containerize full stack applications using Docker, facilitating consistent environments and easier deployment.

Orchestration with Kubernetes: Proficiency in deploying and managing containerized applications using Kubernetes, enabling automated scaling and management.

Load Balancing and Auto-Scaling: Understanding of implementing load balancers and configuring auto-scaling to handle increased traffic and ensure application resilience.

Scalable Architecture Principles: Knowledge of designing and maintaining scalable full stack architectures, incorporating best practices to support growth and high availability.

Journal Exercises

1. **Docker and Kubernetes:** Containerize your full stack application using Docker and deploy it using Kubernetes. What benefits do these technologies provide in terms of scalability and management?

_____

_____

_____

_____

_____

_____

_____

_____

2. **Load Balancing Implementation:** Set up a load balancer for your application. How does load balancing contribute to handling increased traffic and ensuring high availability?

_____

_____

_____

_____

_____

_____

_____

3. **Auto-Scaling Configuration:** Configure auto-scaling for your application services. Reflect on how auto-

scaling responds to varying loads and maintains application performance.

_____

_____

_____

_____

_____

_____

_____

_____

4. **Scalable Architecture Design:** Evaluate your application's architecture for scalability. What best practices did you implement to ensure your application can handle growth?

_____

_____

_____

_____

NOTE

PART 6

REAL-WORLD PROJECT

CHAPTER 16

BUILDING A FULL STACK APPLICATION

This chapter provides a step-by-step guide to building a full stack **Task Management App**. The application includes a Spring Boot backend for managing tasks, a React frontend for user interactions, and secure authentication and authorization for user access control.

Project Overview: A Task Management App

1. Application Features

- **User Registration and Authentication**: Users can register, log in, and manage their tasks securely.

- **Task Management**: Users can create, read, update, and delete tasks.

- **Role-Based Authorization**: Only authorized users can access specific features.

- **Responsive Design**: The frontend is optimized for desktop and mobile devices.

2. Tech Stack

- **Backend**: Spring Boot with JPA and H2 (or any SQL database).
- **Frontend**: React with Context API for state management.
- **Authentication**: JWT (JSON Web Tokens).
- **Deployment**: Dockerized backend and React hosted on Netlify or Vercel.

Backend: Designing and Building REST APIs

1. Set Up Spring Boot Project

Dependencies:

Add the following to `pom.xml`:

```xml
<dependency>
    <groupId>org.springframework.boot</groupId>
    <artifactId>spring-boot-starter-web</artifactId>
</dependency>
<dependency>
    <groupId>org.springframework.boot</groupId>
```

```xml
        <artifactId>spring-boot-starter-data-
jpa</artifactId>
</dependency>
<dependency>
    <groupId>org.springframework.boot</groupId>
    <artifactId>spring-boot-starter-
security</artifactId>
</dependency>
<dependency>
    <groupId>io.jsonwebtoken</groupId>
    <artifactId>jjwt-api</artifactId>
    <version>0.11.5</version>
</dependency>
<dependency>
    <groupId>com.h2database</groupId>
    <artifactId>h2</artifactId>
    <scope>runtime</scope>
</dependency>
```

2. Create Database Entities

User Entity:

```java
import jakarta.persistence.Entity;
import jakarta.persistence.GeneratedValue;
import jakarta.persistence.GenerationType;
import jakarta.persistence.Id;
import java.util.Set;

@Entity
public class User {
    @Id
    @GeneratedValue(strategy = GenerationType.IDENTITY)
    private Long id;
    private String username;
    private String password;
    private String role;

    // Getters and Setters
}
```

Task Entity:

```java
import jakarta.persistence.Entity;
import jakarta.persistence.GeneratedValue;
import jakarta.persistence.GenerationType;
import jakarta.persistence.Id;

@Entity
public class Task {
```

```java
    @Id
    @GeneratedValue(strategy = GenerationType.IDENTITY)
    private Long id;
    private String title;
    private String description;
    private boolean completed;


    // Getters and Setters
}
```

3. Build REST APIs

User Controller:

```java
import org.springframework.web.bind.annotation.*;

@RestController
@RequestMapping("/users")
public class UserController {
    // User registration logic
    @PostMapping("/register")
    public String registerUser(@RequestBody User
user) {
        // Save user logic
        return "User registered successfully";
    }
```

```
}
```

xTask Controller:

```java
import org.springframework.web.bind.annotation.*;
import java.util.List;

@RestController
@RequestMapping("/tasks")
public class TaskController {
    @GetMapping
    public List<Task> getAllTasks() {
        // Logic to fetch all tasks
    }

    @PostMapping
    public Task createTask(@RequestBody Task task) {
        // Logic to create a new task
    }
}
```

Frontend: Creating React Components and Managing State

1. Set Up React Project

Initialize the React app and install dependencies:

```
npx create-react-app task-app
npm install axios react-router-dom
```

2. Create Components

TaskList Component

Displays a list of tasks.

```
import React, { useState, useEffect } from 'react';
import axios from 'axios';

function TaskList() {
    const [tasks, setTasks] = useState([]);

    useEffect(() => {
        axios.get('/api/tasks')
            .then((response)                            =>
setTasks(response.data))
            .catch((error) => console.error(error));
    }, []);

    return (
        <ul>
            {tasks.map((task) => (
                <li key={task.id}>{task.title}</li>
            ))}
```

```
        </ul>
    );
}


export default TaskList;
```

TaskForm Component

Allows users to create or update tasks.

```
import React, { useState } from 'react';
import axios from 'axios';


function TaskForm() {
    const [title, setTitle] = useState('');
    const      [description,      setDescription]      =
useState('');


    const handleSubmit = (e) => {
        e.preventDefault();
        axios.post('/api/tasks',          {          title,
description })
            .then((response)                             =>
console.log(response.data))
            .catch((error) => console.error(error));
    };
```

```
    return (
        <form onSubmit={handleSubmit}>
            <input
                type="text"
                placeholder="Task Title"
                value={title}
                onChange={(e)                        =>
setTitle(e.target.value)}
            />
            <textarea
                placeholder="Task Description"
                value={description}
                onChange={(e)                        =>
setDescription(e.target.value)}
            />
            <button type="submit">Add Task</button>
        </form>
    );
}


export default TaskForm;
```

Connecting Backend and Frontend

1. Set Up Proxy for API Requests

Add a proxy in **package.json** to route frontend requests to the backend during development:

```
"proxy": "http://localhost:8080"
```

2. Axios for API Requests

Example: Fetch tasks:

```
axios.get('/tasks')
    .then(response => console.log(response.data))
    .catch(error => console.error(error));
```

Adding Authentication and Authorization

1. Backend: JWT Authentication

Generate JWT Tokens:

```
import io.jsonwebtoken.Jwts;
import io.jsonwebtoken.SignatureAlgorithm;

public class JwtUtil {
    private final String SECRET_KEY = "secret";

    public String generateToken(String username) {
```

```
        return Jwts.builder()
            .setSubject(username)
            .signWith(SignatureAlgorithm.HS256,
SECRET_KEY)
            .compact();
    }
}
```

Authenticate Users:

```
@PostMapping("/login")
public String login(@RequestBody User user) {
    // Validate user credentials
    return
jwtUtil.generateToken(user.getUsername());
}
```

2. Frontend: Manage Tokens

Store JWT in local storage or cookies.

Login Component:

```
import React, { useState } from 'react';
import axios from 'axios';

function Login() {
```

```
    const [username, setUsername] = useState('');
    const [password, setPassword] = useState('');

    const handleLogin = (e) => {
        e.preventDefault();
        axios.post('/api/users/login', { username,
password })
            .then((response) => {
                localStorage.setItem('token',
response.data.token);
            })
            .catch((error) => console.error(error));
    };

    return (
        <form onSubmit={handleLogin}>
            <input
                type="text"
                placeholder="Username"
                value={username}
                onChange={(e)                        =>
setUsername(e.target.value)}
            />
            <input
                type="password"
```

```
                 placeholder="Password"
                 value={password}
                 onChange={(e)                              =>
setPassword(e.target.value)}
            />
            <button type="submit">Login</button>
        </form>
    );
}

export default Login;
```

Summary

In this chapter, you built a comprehensive full stack **Task Management App**. You designed a Spring Boot backend with REST APIs, created a React frontend with components and state management, connected the frontend and backend seamlessly, and added JWT-based authentication and role-based authorization. This workflow equips you to develop robust full stack applications.

Key Takeaways

Project Overview: Comprehensive understanding of planning and executing a full stack application project, focusing on a Task Management App as a case study.

Authentication and Authorization: Practical experience in integrating secure authentication and authorization mechanisms to protect application resources and user data.

End-to-End Development: Skills in developing and managing the complete lifecycle of a full stack application, from initial setup to feature implementation.

Journal Exercises

1. **Project Planning:** Outline the key features and requirements of your Task Management App. How did you prioritize functionalities during development?

_____

_____

_____

_____

_____

_____

_____

_____

2. **Authentication and Authorization Implementation:**
Implement authentication and authorization in your
application. What security measures did you
integrate to protect user data?

_____

_____

_____

_____

_____

_____

_____

3. **Feature Development:** Document the development process of a core feature in your Task Management App. What challenges did you encounter, and how did you overcome them?

_____

_____

_____

_____

_____

_____

_____

CHAPTER 17

ENHANCING THE APPLICATION

In this chapter, our focus is on enhancing the functionality, performance, and deployment readiness of the **Task Management App**. Topics include adding advanced features like **notifications** and **file uploads**, optimizing performance through tuning and testing, and deploying the full stack application.

Adding Advanced Features

1. Real-Time Notifications

Notifications can improve user experience by providing instant updates about key events (e.g., task assignments, status changes).

Backend: WebSocket Integration

Add **Dependencies**:

Include Spring WebSocket in `pom.xml`:

```
<dependency>
    <groupId>org.springframework.boot</groupId>
```

```
    <artifactId>spring-boot-starter-
websocket</artifactId>
</dependency>
```

WebSocket Configuration:

```
import
org.springframework.context.annotation.Configuration
;
import
org.springframework.messaging.simp.config.MessageBro
kerRegistry;
import
org.springframework.web.socket.config.annotation.Ena
bleWebSocketMessageBroker;
import
org.springframework.web.socket.config.annotation.Sto
mpEndpointRegistry;
import
org.springframework.web.socket.config.annotation.Web
SocketMessageBrokerConfigurer;

@Configuration
@EnableWebSocketMessageBroker
```

```java
public      class      WebSocketConfig      implements
WebSocketMessageBrokerConfigurer {

    @Override
    public                                              void
registerStompEndpoints(StompEndpointRegistry
registry) {

registry.addEndpoint("/ws").setAllowedOrigins("http:
//localhost:3000").withSockJS();
    }

    @Override
    public                                              void
configureMessageBroker(MessageBrokerRegistry
registry) {
        registry.enableSimpleBroker("/topic");

registry.setApplicationDestinationPrefixes("/app");
    }
}
```

Broadcast Notifications:

```
import
org.springframework.messaging.simp.SimpMessagingTemp
late;
import org.springframework.stereotype.Service;

@Service
public class NotificationService {

    private         final        SimpMessagingTemplate
messagingTemplate;

    public NotificationService(SimpMessagingTemplate
messagingTemplate) {
        this.messagingTemplate = messagingTemplate;
    }

    public void sendNotification(String message) {

messagingTemplate.convertAndSend("/topic/notificatio
ns", message);
    }
}
```

Frontend: Real-Time Notification Display

Install WebSocket Libraries:

```
npm install sockjs-client @stomp/stompjs
```

Connect to WebSocket:

```
import React, { useEffect } from 'react';
import { over } from '@stomp/stompjs';
import SockJS from 'sockjs-client';

const Notifications = () => {
    useEffect(() => {
        const          socket          =          new
SockJS('http://localhost:8080/ws');
        const stompClient = over(socket);

        stompClient.connect({}, () => {

stompClient.subscribe('/topic/notifications',
(message) => {

console.log(JSON.parse(message.body));
        });
      });
    }, []);
```

```
    return <div>Real-Time Notifications</div>;
};


export default Notifications;
```

2. File Uploads

Allow users to attach files (e.g., documents, images) to tasks.

Backend: File Upload Endpoint

Add File Upload Logic:

```
import org.springframework.web.bind.annotation.*;
import
org.springframework.web.multipart.MultipartFile;

import java.io.File;
import java.io.IOException;

@RestController
@RequestMapping("/files")
public class FileController {

    @PostMapping("/upload")
```

```java
    public String uploadFile(@RequestParam("file")
MultipartFile file) throws IOException {
        File destination = new File("uploads/" +
file.getOriginalFilename());
        file.transferTo(destination);
        return "File uploaded successfully: " +
destination.getAbsolutePath();
    }
}
```

Enable Multipart Config:

Add to **application.properties**:

```properties
spring.servlet.multipart.max-file-size=10MB
spring.servlet.multipart.max-request-size=10MB
```

Frontend: File Upload Form

File Upload Component:

```jsx
import React, { useState } from 'react';
import axios from 'axios';

const FileUpload = () => {
    const [file, setFile] = useState(null);
```

```
    const        handleFileChange       =        (e)       =>
setFile(e.target.files[0]);


    const handleUpload = () => {
        const formData = new FormData();
        formData.append('file', file);


        axios.post('/api/files/upload', formData, {
            headers:            {            'Content-Type':
'multipart/form-data' },
        })
            .then((response)                           =>
console.log(response.data))
            .catch((error) => console.error(error));
    };


    return (
        <div>
            <input                            type="file"
onChange={handleFileChange} />
            <button
onClick={handleUpload}>Upload</button>
        </div>
    );
};
```

```
export default FileUpload;
```

Performance Tuning and Testing

1. Backend Performance Optimization

1. **Database Indexing**:

   Add indexes to frequently queried columns:

   ```sql
   CREATE INDEX idx_task_title ON tasks(title);
   ```

2. **Query Optimization**:

   Use projections or DTOs to fetch only required

   fields.

3. **Enable Caching**:

   Use Spring Cache for caching API responses.

   ```java
   @Cacheable("tasks")
   public List<Task> getTasks() {
   return taskRepository.findAll();
   }
   ```

2. Frontend Performance Optimization

1. **Lazy Loading**:

   Load components only when needed using

   `React.lazy`.

```
const       TaskList       =       React.lazy(()       =>
import('./TaskList'));


<React.Suspense
fallback={<div>Loading...</div>}>
<TaskList />
</React.Suspense>
```

2. **Code Splitting**:

   Use tools like Webpack to split the bundle into smaller chunks.

3. **Minify Assets**:

   Run `npm run build` to optimize JavaScript and CSS files for production.

3. Testing the Application

1. **Backend Testing**:

   - Write unit and integration tests for APIs.

- Use tools like Postman to manually test endpoints.

2. **Frontend Testing**:
   - Test React components using Jest and React Testing Library.

3. **End-to-End Testing**:
   Use Cypress or Selenium for full stack testing

Deploying the Application

1. Backend Deployment

Option 1: Dockerize the Backend

Create a `Dockerfile`:

```
FROM openjdk:17-jdk-slim
WORKDIR /app
COPY target/myapp.jar app.jar
EXPOSE 8080
ENTRYPOINT ["java", "-jar", "app.jar"]
```

Build and Push the Image:

```
docker build -t myapp .
docker tag myapp myregistry/myapp
docker push myregistry/myapp
```

Option 2: Deploy to AWS Elastic Beanstalk

1. Upload the JAR file.
2. Configure environment variables.
3. Use Amazon RDS for the database.

---

2. Frontend Deployment

Deploy to Netlify

Build the React app:

```
npm run build
```

Drag and drop the `build` folder to Netlify or link the GitHub repository.

3. Integrating Frontend and Backend

Set up a **reverse proxy** (e.g., NGINX) to route traffic to the appropriate service.

Use **environment variables** in React for backend API URLs.

Add a `.env` file:

```
REACT_APP_API_URL=https://api.myapp.com
```

Summary

In this chapter, we enhanced the **Task Management App** by adding advanced features like real-time notifications and file uploads. We also covered performance tuning techniques and deployment strategies for both the backend and frontend. With these additions, the application is now production-ready and scalable for a wide audience.

Key Takeaways

Real-Time Features: Ability to enhance applications with real-time functionalities, such as notifications, using WebSockets or similar technologies.

Production Deployment: Knowledge of deploying enhanced applications to production environments, ensuring reliability, performance, and scalability.

Continuous Improvement: Understanding the importance of user feedback in refining and improving application features and overall user experience.

Journal Exercises

1. **Real-Time Notifications:** Add real-time notification features to your Task Management App. How did you implement real-time updates, and what technologies did you use?

_____

_____

_____

_____

_____

_____

_____

2. **Deployment Strategies:** Deploy the enhanced application to a production environment. What steps did you take to ensure a smooth deployment, and how did you test the deployed application?

_____

_____

_____

_____

_____

_____

_____

_____

3. **User Feedback Integration:** Gather feedback from potential users. How did you incorporate this feedback to improve the application's functionality and user experience?

_____

_____

CONCLUSION

This book has provided a comprehensive journey through building, deploying, and scaling full stack applications using **Spring Boot** and **React**. Let's conclude by recapping the key concepts, outlining the next steps in your full stack development journey, and recommending resources for continuous learning.

Recap of Key Concepts

1. Full Stack Fundamentals

- **Frontend**: React was used to create dynamic and user-friendly interfaces, leveraging state management, routing, and component-based architecture.

- **Backend**: Spring Boot provided a robust framework for building scalable and secure REST APIs with essential features like JPA for database interaction and Spring Security for authentication and authorization.

2. Integration of Frontend and Backend

- **RESTful APIs**: Established seamless communication between the frontend and backend.
- **Authentication**: Implemented JWT-based security to protect APIs and ensure proper user role access.
- **State Management**: Used React's Context API for handling application state efficiently.

3. Advanced Features and Enhancements

- **Real-Time Updates**: Introduced WebSockets for real-time notifications.
- **File Uploads**: Enabled users to upload and manage files effectively.
- **Performance Optimization**: Applied techniques like caching, lazy loading, and database indexing to enhance application performance.

4. Deployment and Scaling

- **Frontend**: Hosted React applications on platforms like Netlify and Vercel for fast and reliable deployment.
- **Backend**: Leveraged cloud providers such as AWS, Azure, and Heroku, and orchestrated microservices using Docker and Kubernetes.
- **Scaling**: Implemented load balancers and auto-scaling to handle increased user traffic.

Next Steps in Full Stack Development

1. Explore Advanced Backend Topics

- **Microservices Architecture**: Expand on the principles of distributed systems, using tools like Spring Cloud and Kafka.
- **Event-Driven Design**: Learn to implement asynchronous processing with message brokers like RabbitMQ or Apache Kafka.
- **GraphQL APIs**: Explore GraphQL for flexible and efficient data querying.

2. Enhance Frontend Skills

- **React Ecosystem**: Dive deeper into tools like Redux, Recoil, or Zustand for advanced state management.
- **Next.js**: Learn server-side rendering and static site generation with this React-based framework.
- **Frontend Performance**: Optimize rendering with React's memoization, virtualization libraries, and progressive web apps (PWAs).

3. Master Cloud and DevOps

- **CI/CD Pipelines**: Automate testing, builds, and deployments using Jenkins, GitHub Actions, or GitLab CI/CD.
- **Serverless Computing**: Explore AWS Lambda or Azure Functions to build lightweight, event-driven services.

- **Monitoring and Logging**: Use tools like Prometheus, Grafana, and ELK stack to monitor and debug production systems.

4. Contribute to Open Source

Participate in open-source projects to learn best practices, improve coding skills, and network with other developers.

Recommended Resources for Continuous Learning

Books

1. **Backend**:

   Spring Microservices in Action by John Carnell.

   Clean Architecture: A Craftsman's Guide to Software Structure and Design by Robert C. Martin.

2. **Frontend**:

   React Up & Running by Stoyan Stefanov.

   Learning React by Alex Banks and Eve Porcello.

3. **Full Stack**:

Full Stack Development with Spring Boot and React by Juha Hinkula.

Online Courses and Platforms

1.Frontend Development:

- Frontend Masters
- Scrimba's React Course

2.Backend Development:

- Spring Framework Tutorials
- Baeldung's Spring Boot Course

3.Full Stack Development:

- Coursera Full Stack Specializations
- Pluralsight

Communities and Forums

1. **Stack Overflow**: Get help for specific technical problems.
2. **GitHub**: Contribute to projects and collaborate with developers.

3. **Reddit**: Join subreddits like `r/learnprogramming`, `r/javascript`, or `r/springboot`.

Tools for Practice

- **LeetCode** and **HackerRank**: For coding challenges and algorithm practice.
- **CodePen** and **JSFiddle**: For frontend experiments.
- **Postman** and **Swagger**: For API testing and documentation.

Final Thoughts

Becoming proficient in full stack development requires continuous learning, hands-on practice, and a passion for solving real-world problems. This book has equipped you with foundational and advanced concepts to create robust, scalable applications. Keep building, experimenting, and pushing your boundaries—because the best way to learn is by doing.

Happy coding! 🚀

NOTE

APPENDICES

Appendix A: Full Stack Development Tools and Resources

- Overview of Commonly Used Tools in Full Stack Development
- Official Documentation for Spring Boot 3 and React
- Popular IDEs for JavaScript and Java Development
- Recommended Courses and Tutorials for Further Learning

Appendix B: Sample Code for Common Use Cases

- Example of a Basic Spring Boot Application
- Sample React Components and State Management
- Custom API Security with JWT Authentication
- Connecting React and Spring Boot Using Axios

Appendix C: Troubleshooting and FAQs

- Solving Common Spring Boot 3 Issues
- Fixing React Development Errors
- Understanding CORS Errors and Solutions
- How to Handle Deployment Issues

Appendix D: Full Stack Development Best Practices

- Best Practices for Writing Clean and Maintainable Code
- Managing Complex Application States in React
- Optimizing Backend Services with Spring Boot
- Security Best Practices in Full Stack Development

Appendix E: Quick Reference for Spring Boot 3 and React

- Frequently Used Spring Boot Annotations
- Commonly Used React Hooks
- Key Spring Boot Configuration Properties
- React Component Lifecycle Methods

www.ingramcontent.com/pod-product-compliance
Lightning Source LLC
LaVergne TN
LVHW012334060326
832902LV00012B/1879